My AMIGURUMI TOYS

16 AMIGURUMI PATTERNS TO CROCHET

LANA CHOI

Tuva Publishing
www.tuvapublishing.com

Address Merkez Mah. Cavusbasi Cad. No71
Cekmekoy - Istanbul 34782 / Turkey
Tel +9 0216 642 62 62

My Amigurumi Toys

First Print July / 2022

All Global Copyrights Belong To
Tuva Tekstil ve Yayıncılık Ltd.

Content Crochet

Editor in Chief Ayhan DEMİRPEHLİVAN
Project Editor Kader DEMİRPEHLİVAN
Author Lana CHOI
Technical Editors Leyla ARAS
Crochet Tech Editors Wendi CUSINS
Graphic Designers Ömer ALP, Abdullah BAYRAKÇI,
Tarık TOKGÖZ
Photograph Lana CHOI, Tuva Publishing

ISBN 978-605-7834-51-5

 TuvaYayincilik    TuvaPublishing

 TuvaYayincilik    TuvaPublishing

CONTENTS

GET READY?
××× BEFORE MAKING YOUR DOLL FRIENDS ×××

PROJECT GALLERY

ALBERT & BERTHA THE WEDDING BEARS
P.36

SAM & PAM THE TWINS
P.46

LOGAN & LAURA THE YOUNG COUPLE
P.56

ROBERT THE RABBIT
P.68

HARRY THE HAPPY PUPPY
P.74

ROCKY ROOSTER AND THE CHICKLETS
P.82

KENNETH CARROT & BENJAMIN BROCCOLI
THE SMART VEGATABLES P.92

ZACK & ZOE THE CUTE COUPLE
P.100

DYLAN & DAOTA THE TALL COUPLE
P.110

INTRODUCTION

I work as an optician in Korea. In 2013, I started making Amigurumi because I fell in love with the Amineko (a crocheted cat toy), which a customer had brought along to my office.

The idea of making a toy, with only a hook and some yarn, was very appealing to me. No special tools needed and you can work on it anywhere. What a pleasure!

The toys started piling up as I was making something new every day. My husband then built a display area for them in the one corner of the outer office.

I was having so much fun making Amigurumi that I wanted to share my new passion. Soon I started designing patterns and teaching others how to make these little toys - to show them that anyone can create something beautiful quite easily, and enjoy doing it!

Through social media, I discovered that many people from all over the world like my Amigurumi designs. Working with my good partner, Tuva Publishing, we have put together a wonderful book containing 16 of my favorite Amigurumi friends which I'd like to share and make along with you.

Allow me to introduce you to:

Albert & Bertha - a lovely bear couple on their wedding day.
Sam & Pam - a twin brother and sister, who love doing things together.
Logan & Laura - a friendly young couple taking a walk outdoors.
Robert, a brave rabbit, and Harry, a happy puppy - will go anywhere with you.
Rocky Rooster and his clutch of cute chicks following him around.
From a diligent farmer, we have Kenneth Carrot and Benjamin Broccoli.
Zack & Zoë - cute little kids who are excited to start their new school.
Dylan & Dakota – a really tall couple who enjoy sitting in the corner of my bed.

I hope each and every one of my Amigurumi friends will bring you joy whenever you make them.

Lana from Incheon, Korea

BASICS

Materials & Tools

Yarn

Cotton Yarn is the preferred choice to use when making dolls. I used Hello Cotton yarn for the toys in this book.

Note: Medium Weight (Worsted) yarn or Light Weight (DK) yarn is suitable for the projects.

Crochet Hooks

Crochet Hook No.5/0 (3.00mm)

Crochet Hook No.4/0 (2.50mm)

Crochet Hook No.3/0 (2.25mm)

For the dolls, it is important to crochet tightly so that the stuffing doesn't come out. Use a hook which is size or two smaller than the hook size recommended on the yarn label.

Yarn Needles

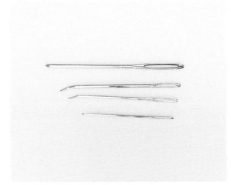

A selection of different sized tapestry needles is needed for both finishing off and assembling the various parts of the dolls.

Yarn Weight	Yarn Types
1 SUPER FINE	Sock, Fingering, Baby
2 FINE	Sport, Baby
3 LIGHT	DK, Light Worsted
4 MEDIUM	Worsted, Afghan, Aran
5 BULKY	Chunky, Craft, Rug

Metric	US	UK	Japan
2.25 mm	B-1	13	3/0
2.50 mm	-	12	4/0
2.75 mm	C-2	-	
3.00 mm	-	11	5/0
3.25 mm	D-3	10	
3.50 mm	E-4	9	6/0
3.75 mm	F-5	-	
4.00 mm	G-6	8	7/0
4.50 mm	#7	7	7.5/0
5.00 mm	H-8	6	8/0

Straight Pins

These are used to either mark the exact location before sewing, or to secure pieces together.

Locking Stitch Markers

These handy markers are used to mark the beginning stitch of each round, or to mark off a number of stitches.

Water-Soluble Marking Pen

The marks made with this pen are easily removed with water, making it useful to mark the position on each piece before assembling.

Forceps

These are used to insert the stuffing into deep narrow spaces where it is difficult to use your fingers, especially all the way into the tips of the feet and arms.

Sharp Pointed Tweezers

This can be used instead of the forceps when stuffing the doll. They are also used to hide the yarn tails inside the doll.

Buttons

These are used as the eyes or nose on the faces of the dolls. Depending on the size and shape of the buttons, you can change the whole expression and mood of the doll. They are also used to decorate the dolls.

Bean Button

These are also used as the eyes or nose of a doll to create different expressions. They're called bean buttons, because they look like beans.

Toy Stuffing

When making the dolls, it is a good idea to use stuffing that does not clump together. It should hold its shape well and be suitable (and safe) for children.

Scissors

These are needed to cut and trim the yarn and threads, as well as to cut out felt or fabric shapes. Make sure they are sharp enough to cut through the yarn cleanly.

Sewing Thread

Used for embroidering facial features on the dolls, and to sew on buttons. I use a thread which is thicker and stronger than normal thread, which is more suitable when sewing on crochet fabric.

Sewing Needles

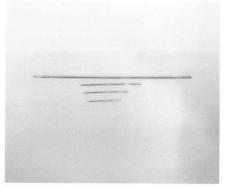

These are used with the sewing threads. The different sizes and lengths are for the various purposes needed for the dolls.

Craft Wire

When this is used inside the dolls, the arms and legs are bendable. However, if the doll is for a young child, please do not use wire.

How to Hold a Crochet Hook

Pencil Hold

With the hook pointing down, hold the hook with your middle finger and thumb, as if it were a pencil.

Knife Hold

With the hook pointing down, hold the hook with your index finger extended, as if you were holding a knife.

How to Hold the Yarn

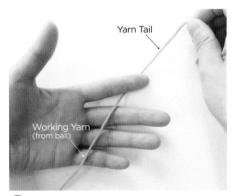

Yarn Tail

Working Yarn (from ball)

1. Place the yarn across your left hand with the yarn tail under your index finger.

2. Wrap the yarn tail over your index finger and hold the working yarn with your left hand ring finger.

3. Hold the tail between your thumb and middle finger. Adjust the tension of the yarn by bending and flexing the index finger.

How to Wrap the Yarn Over the Hook

1. Place the hook in front of the yarn.

2. Move the hook under the yarn and upwards in a circular motion, so that the yarn wraps around the hook.

3. Pull the yarn through the loop on the hook. Use this method to wrap the yarn for every crochet stitch.

Finding the Correct Hook for the Yarn

Finding the correct hook size to match the thickness of the yarn is important when crocheting toys. Generally, one would choose a hook one or two sizes smaller than that recommended on the yarn label, so that a tighter fabric is created. However, because each person works at a different tension, and each yarn company uses different standards to determine the hook sizes, it is a good idea to work up yarn swatches before making the dolls. Work the swatches using different sized hooks – larger and smaller - than what you would normally use, and compare the results, before making a doll.

» Using a 4.00 mm hook

» Using a 3.00 mm hook

» Using a 2.25 mm hook

Using a larger hook with the yarn, the crochet piece stretches easily. Holes are formed between the stitches, where the stuffing can easily come out.

Here the crochet piece does not stretch well. Stitches are formed tightly with no visible holes between them.

Using a smaller hook, the fabric is denser and feels stiff.

4.00 mm
Crochet Hook

3.00 mm
Crochet Hook

2.25 mm
Crochet Hook

HELLO
76 COLOURS

ART.C25
+/- 25G - 62.5M - 68YDS
76 COLOURS

ART.C50
+/- 50G - 125M - 136YDS
76 COLOURS

3
10x10cm / 4"x4"
2.5 - 3.5

10x10cm / 4"x4"
2.5
27
24

161	114	125	137	153
162	115	126	138	154
163	116	127	139	155
101	117	128	140	156
102	118	129	141	173
103	119	130	142	157
104	120	169	143	158
105	121	170	144	174
106	122	131	145	159
107	123	133	146	175
108	164	134	147	176
109	124	132	148	160
110	165	171	149	
111	166	135	150	
112	167	136	151	
113	168	172	152	

CONFIDENCE IN TEXTILES
Tested for harmful substances
according to Oeko-Tex Standard 100
15 HTR 73292   HOHENSTEIN HTTI

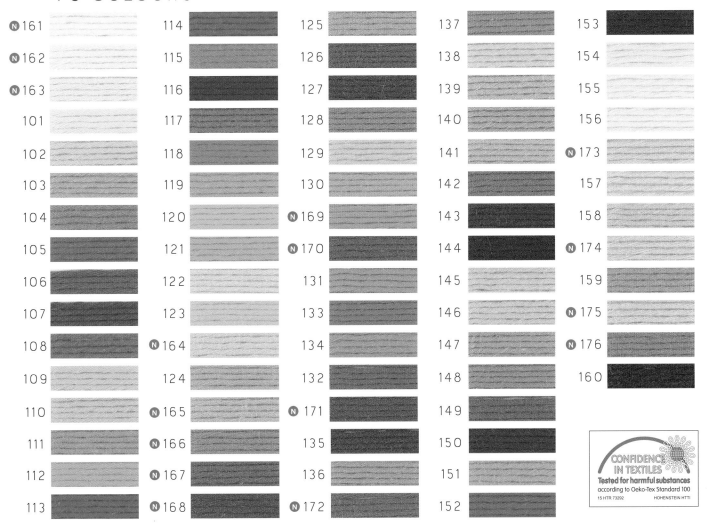

13

◦ BASIC CROCHET STITCHES ◦

CHAIN STITCH (ch)

This stitch is the basis of many crochet projects. It is used as a foundation when working in rows or when making ovals. It is good to practice this stitch.

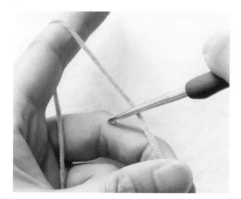

1 Place the hook on the yarn.

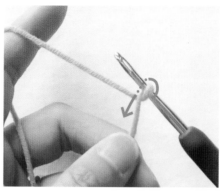

2 Turn the hook downwards under the yarn, and then lift the hook up to form a loop on the hook.

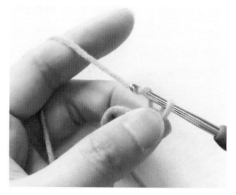

3 Hold the twist in the yarn tightly with your thumb and middle finger, and wrap the yarn over the hook.

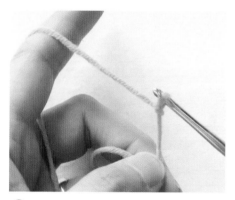

4 Pull the wrapped yarn through the loop on the hook to make a knot. This is not the first chain stitch.

5 Wrap the yarn over the hook and pull the wrapped yarn through the loop on the hook to make the first chain stitch.

6 Repeat this process to make as many chain stitches as you need. In the photo, there are 10 chain stitches made.

tip

Chain Front: The shape of a "V" is at the front of a chain stitch.

Back Ridge: An arch shape is on the back of a chain stitch.

Chain Front

Back Ridge

SINGLE CROCHET (sc)

This is the stitch most used when crocheting dolls. It is also the most suitable stitch to use because of its tight structure. It is used to form the overall shape of every doll's body and head, so be sure to learn and practice it.

1 Insert the hook under both loops of the next stitch on the previous round.

2 Wrap the yarn over the hook.

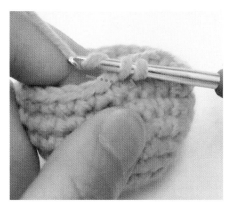

③ Pull the wrapped yarn through the stitch to make a loop. There are now two loops on the hook.

④ Wrap the yarn over the hook again. Pull the yarn through the two loops on the hook to complete the single crochet stitch.

⑤ Repeat the process in steps 1-4 for every single crochet stitch, as many times as necessary. The photo shows 5 single crochet stitches.

BACK LOOP ONLY (blo)

Working in the back loop only is a technique often used in stitch patterns, where the hook in inserted only in the back loop of a stitch instead of under both loops of the stitch. The process of making the stitch is the same, only where the hook gets inserted is different. If you are confused, please refer to the Single Crochet explanation.

① The colored part is where to insert the hook.

② Insert the hook into the back loop only of the next stitch on the previous round.

③ Wrap the yarn over the hook and pull it through the back loop.

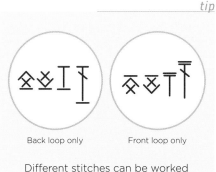

tip

④ Wrap the yarn over the hook again and pull it through the two loops on the hook to complete a back loop only single crochet stitch.

⑤ Repeat the process in steps 2-4 as many times as necessary. The photo shows a round of back loop only stitches completed. You can see a horizontal line (formed by the unused front loops) under the current round.

Back loop only   Front loop only

Different stitches can be worked in the back loop only or front loop only, including decreases, increases and other basic crochet stitches.

FRONT LOOP ONLY (flo)

This technique is used when you need your work to fold outwards, or have a shaped part, like a visor on a hat. Working in the front loop only is where the hook is inserted under the front loop of a stitch. Please note that this technique can be used with various crochet stitches.

1 The colored part is where to insert the hook.

2 Insert the hook into the front loop only of the next stitch on the previous round.

3 Pull the yarn through the front loop.

4 Wrap the yarn over the hook again and pull it through the two loops on the hook to complete the stitch.

5 Repeat the process in steps 2-4 as many times as needed. The photos show a round of front loop only stitches completed. On the inside, you can see the horizontal line (formed by unused back loops) under the last round.

SINGLE CROCHET INCREASE (sc-inc or 2sc)

This is a crochet technique that increases the number of stitches so that the total area of the doll becomes larger as you progress. Working another single crochet stitch into the same stitch, increases one stitch to two stitches.

1 Complete 1 single crochet.

2 Insert the hook into the same stitch and work one more single crochet.

3 When that is done, it shows the 2 single crochets worked into the 1 stitch. You can see the 1 stitch extended at the end.

SINGLE CROCHET DECREASE (sc-dec or sc2tog)

This is how to reduce two stitches to one stitch. We'll show you both the normal decrease and the invisible decrease, which is more suitable for doll making, so practice both ways.

» A Normal Decrease

1 Insert the hook into the next stitch on the previous round.

2 Wrap the yarn over the hook and pull the wrapped yarn through the stitch to make a loop. There are now two loops on the hook.

3 Then insert the hook in the following stitch, wrap the yarn over the hook and pull the wrapped yarn through the stitch. There are now three loops on your hook.

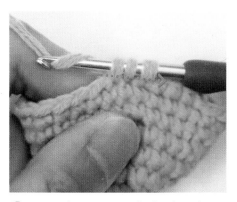

4 Wrap the yarn over the hook and pull through all three loops on hook.

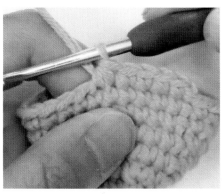

5 After making 4 single crochets, the following 2 stitches were reduced to 1 single crochet.

» Invisible decrease (suitable for making dolls)

1 Insert the hook into the front loop only of the next stitch on the previous round.

2 Then insert the hook under the front loop only of the following stitch and pull the yarn through both these front loops. There are now two loops on the hook.

3 Wrap the yarn over the hook and pull through both loops on hook.

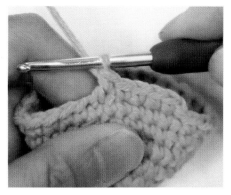

4 After 4 single crochets, the following 2 stitches were reduced to 1 single crochet with an invisible decrease.

BACK POST SINGLE CROCHET (BPsc)

This technique bends the tops of the stitches on the previous round towards you and is achieved by working between the stitches around the post of the stitch.

1 Insert the hook from the back and around the post of the stitch.

2 Wrap the yarn over the hook and pull the wrapped yarn through the stitch post to make a loop. There are now two loops on the hook.

3 Wrap the yarn over the hook again, and pull through both loops on the hook to complete the single crochet.

4 Repeat the process in steps 1-3 for each back post single crochet. The photo shows one round worked in back post single crochet stitches.

tip

Stitch Height: The height of the stitch in terms of chain stiches. The photo shows the height of single crochet (one chain), half-double crochet (two chains), and double crochet (three chains) stitches respectively.

Single Crochet

Half-Double Crochet

Double Crochet

SLIP STITCH (sl st)

When working in rounds, a slip stitch is used to join the last stitch of the round to the first stitch. It can also be used to move across to another stitch position, or to secure the ends when finished crocheting.

» **Joining with a slip stitch**

1 When the last stitch is made, it's time to join to the first stitch to finish the round.

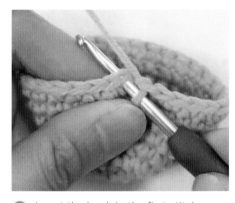

2 Insert the hook in the first stitch.

3 Wrap the yarn over the hook, and pull the yarn through the stitch and through the loop on the hook.

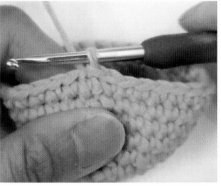

4 The photo shows the finished slip stitch join.

1 Insert the hook in the next stitch.

2 Wrap the yarn over the hook and pull it through the stitch and loop on the hook.

3 The position has been moved by 5 slip stitches.

HALF-DOUBLE CROCHET (hdc)

The height of this stitch is twice as long as the single crochet, and can work up more quickly. However, due to the longer length, there's a chance of the stuffing escaping, so this stitch is used mainly for clothes and accessories.

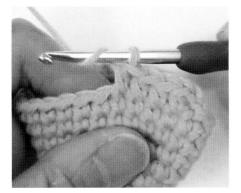

1 Wrap the yarn over the hook.

2 Insert the hook into the next stitch on the previous round.

3 Wrap the yarn over the hook and pull it through the stitch. There are now three loops on the hook.

4 Wrap the yarn over the hook again and pull through all three loops on the hook, to complete a half-double crochet stitch..

5 Repeat steps 1-4 for each half-double crochet as needed. The first photo shows 5 half-double crochet stitches, and the next photo shows a finished round of half-double crochets.

DOUBLE CROCHET (dc)

The height of the double crochet is three times as long as the single crochet. These longer stitches are better suited to use when making clothes and accessories.

 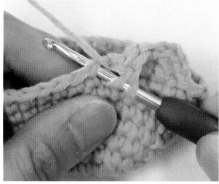 

1. Wrap the yarn over the hook.

2. Insert the hook into the next stitch.

3. Wrap the yarn over the hook and pull it through the stitch. There are now three loops on the hook.

   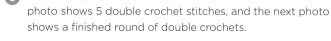

4. Wrap the yarn over the hook and pull it through the first two loops on the hook. There are now two loops left on the hook.

5. Wrap the yarn over the hook once more and pull it through the remaining two loops to complete the double crochet stitch.

6. Repeat steps 1-5 for each double crochet needed. The first photo shows 5 double crochet stitches, and the next photo shows a finished round of double crochets.

DOUBLE CROCHET INCREASE (dc-inc or 2dc)

This crochet technique makes the pieces bigger by increasing the number of stitches. As with the single crochet increase, you can increase the number of double crochet stitches, by working two stitches into one stitch.

 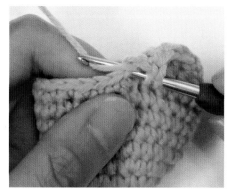 

1. Complete a double crochet stitch. Wrap the yarn over the hook.

2. Insert the hook into the same stitch and work one more double crochet.

3. In the photo, after the first 4 double crochets, there is a double crochet increase. You can see the 1 stitch extended at the end.

DOUBLE CROCHET DECREASE (dc-dec or dc2tog)

This crochet technique reduces two stitches from the previous row into one stitch, using double crochet stitches.

1 Wrap the yarn over the hook.

2 Insert the hook into the next stitch.

3 Wrap the yarn over the hook and pull it through the stitch. There are three loops on the hook.

4 Wrap the yarn over the hook and pull it through the first two loops on the hook. Two loops remain on the hook.

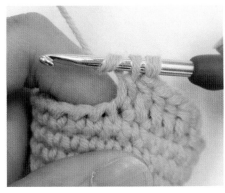

5 Wrap the yarn over the hook again.

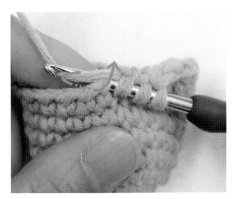

6 Then insert the hook in the following stitch, wrap the yarn over the hook and pull it through the stitch. There are now four loops on your hook.

7 Wrap the yarn over the hook and pull it through the first two loops on the hook.

8 Wrap the yarn over the hook once more and pull it through the remaining three loops on the hook.

9 In the photo, after the first 4 double crochets, there is a double crochet decrease. You can see that 2 stitches on the previous round are now reduced to 1 stitch.

DOUBLE CROCHET SHELL (shell or 5dc-shell)

This crochet technique makes a fan-like shape using double crochet stitches. It looks like a sea shell, so it's called a shell stitch. In this book, it is often used as a decorative border at the bottom of skirts or as hair bangs.

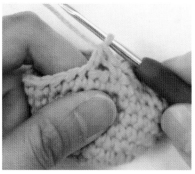

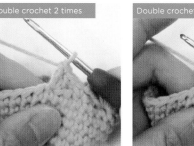

1 After a single crochet stitch is made, wrap the yarn over the hook.

2 Skip the next 2 stitches, insert the hook in the third stitch and make a double crochet stitch. The photo shows one completed double crochet.

3 Make 4 more double crochets in the same stitch. The photos show the series of double crochets made – 2 times, 3 times, 4 times, & 5 times – all in the one stitch.

4 Then skip the next 2 stitches, insert hook in the following stitch and make a single crochet. The single crochet stitches are made before and after each shell.

5 Repeat steps 1-4 for as many shells as needed. The photo shows a finished round of double crochet shell stitches.

○ CROCHET SHAPES ○

WORKING IN ROWS

This is the basic style of crocheting. At the end of each row, change direction and work back across the stitches of the previous row. This style can be used to make flat faces, and in this book is used to make bow ties, ribbons and vest of carrot and broccoli.

1 Make a string of chain stitches (**○**). This is the foundation chain.

2 Add one more chain stitch. This stitch is known as the "turning chain" (**0**) and brings the row up to the height of the stitches. It is not included in the stitch count of the row.

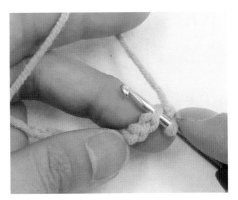

③ Skip the turning chain and insert the hook in the next chain and make a single crochet (✗).

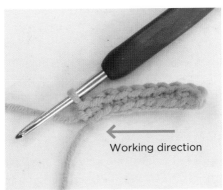

Working direction

④ Work a single crochet in each of the remaining chain stitches to finish the row.

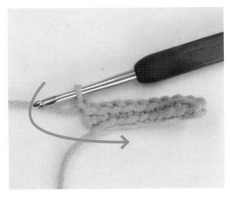

⑤ At the end of the row work one chain stitch (turning chain), and then turn your work around.

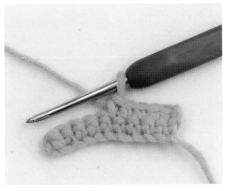

⑥ Insert your hook in the stitch at the base of the turning chain and work a single crochet (✗). Continue working single crochet stitches across the row. Repeat steps 5 & 6 as needed.

⑦ The photo shows the unique pattern created by alternating right side rows and wrong side rows of single crochet stitches.

WORKING IN ROUNDS

This style is most frequently used when making dolls, as it creates a pouch which can be stuffed. There is a formula which needs to be learnt, so practice it well.

» Starting Ring (Magic / Adjustable Ring)

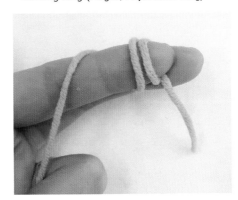

① Wind the yarn tail twice around the index finger on your left hand.

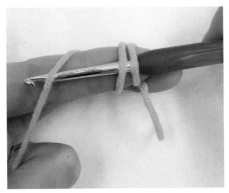

② Insert the hook under the wound yarn and under the working yarn.

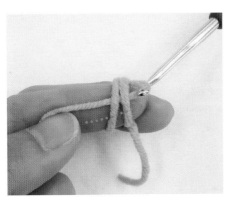

③ Pull the working yarn through, holding the yarn tail between the index and middle finger.

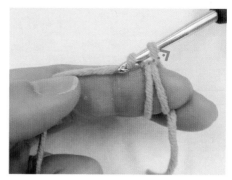

4 Wrap the yarn over the hook and pull it through the loop on hook.

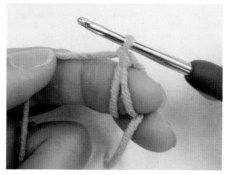

5 The ring is made and you can start crocheting.

» First Round

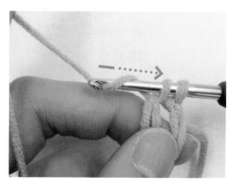

6 Take the ring off your finger carefully.

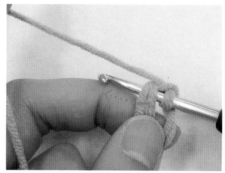

7 With the ring in your left hand, insert the hook into the ring under two strands of yarn.

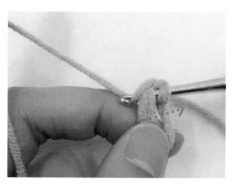

8 Wrap the yarn over the hook and pull it through the ring.

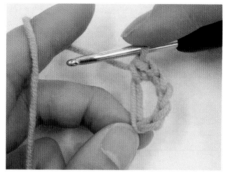

9 Wrap the yarn over the hook again and pull it through both loops on hook to complete a single crochet (**✕**).

10 Repeat steps 7-9 five times more. You have made 6 single crochets.

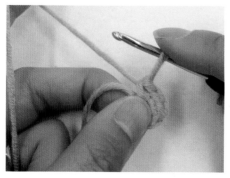

yarn tail

11 Enlarge the working loop on hook and remove hook (taking care not to pull out the stitches). Holding the stitches (with the thumb near the working loop), gently pull the yarn tail to identify which of the two yarn rings is moving.

12 Hold that yarn ring and gently tug the bottom of the ring downwards (away from your thumb) to close the other ring.

13 When the other ring is tightly closed, tug on the yarn tail to close the first ring.

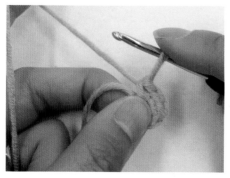

14 Place the hook back in the working loop.

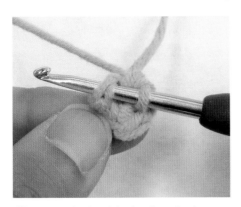

15 Insert the hook in the first single crochet made.

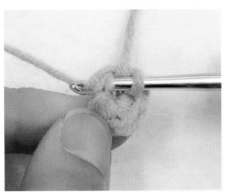

16 Wrap the yarn over the hook and pull the yarn through the stitch and through the loop on the hook to make a slip stitch (●).

17 You have now joined the first round of single crochet stitches with a slip stitch.

» Second Round

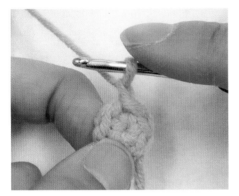

18 To start the round, make one chain stitch, known as the "raising chain" (**0**), to bring the round up to the height of the stitches.

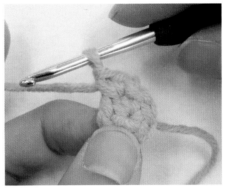

19 Work two single crochet (✗) in the first stitch.

tip

Finding the first stitch of a round: At the end of a round, take care not to work in the chain stitch you made, as this stitch is not included in the stitch count of the round. The next stitch is the first single crochet you made.

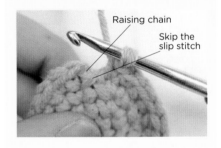

Raising chain
Skip the slip stitch

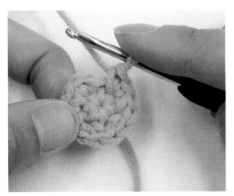

20 Work 2 single crochet stitches in each of the next five stitches – twelve stitches made.

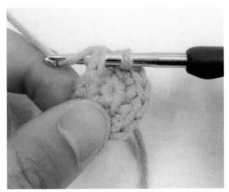

21 Insert the hook in the first single crochet and join with a slip stitch.

22 The photo shows 5 rounds of stitches complete.

MAKING OVALS

This method is created by working stitches around both the top and the bottom side of the foundation chain. It is similar to working in rounds, as each oval round is also joined with a slip stitch. We use this method for making soles of shoes, or the base of a bag.

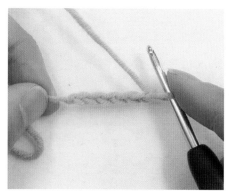

1 Make a foundation chain of 6 stitches (**O**).

2 Add one raising chain (**O**) to bring the row up to height.

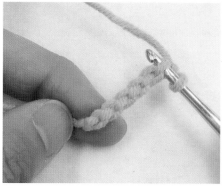

3 Skip the raising chain and insert the hook in the next chain and make a single crochet (**X**).

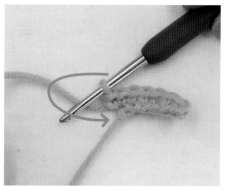

4 Work single crochet stitches in each of the next 4 chains. In the last chain, work 2 single crochets (**⅍**) in the same stitch. Rotate the piece.

5 With the other side of the foundation chain on top, starting in the first chain, work single crochet (**X**) stitches in each of the first 5 chains.

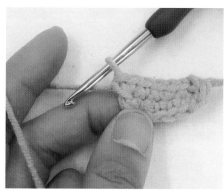

6 In the last chain work 2 single crochets (**⅍**). On each end of the chain is an increase.

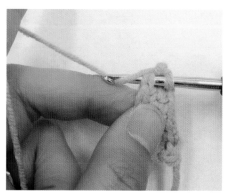

7 Find the first single crochet and join with a slip stitch (•).

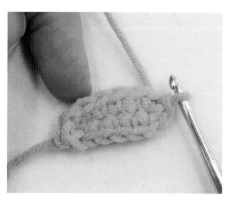

8 The first oval round is finished. The next rounds are similar to working in the round.

9 The photo shows 3 completed oval rounds.

MAKING TUBES

This is used to create circular tubes.

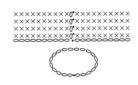

① Make a foundation chain of 20 stitches (**O**).

② Taking care not to twist the stitches, insert the hook in the first chain and make a slip stitch to form a ring. (•).

③ Make one raising chain (**O**). To bring the round up to height.

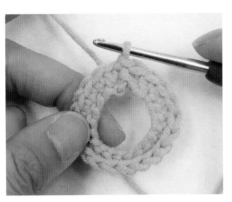

④ Work a single crochet (**X**) in each stitch around. The photo shows the first 5 stitches of the round.

⑤ After finishing the round, join with a slip stitch to the first single crochet.

⑥ Repeat steps 3-5 for as many rounds as needed. The photo shows the first two rounds of a tube.

∘ TECHNIQUES ∘

TIPS!

CHANGING COLORS

This method can also be used to start a new ball of yarn, or when the yarn breaks and you need to rejoin. It is best to change colors at the end of a row or round.

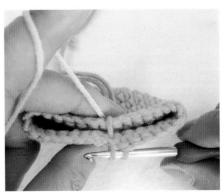

① Before finishing the last stitch of the round, when there are two loops left on the hook.

② Move the yarn to the back of the piece and place the new yarn next to it.

③ Hold the two strands of yarn against the piece with your middle finger and wrap the yarn around the index finger of your left hand, as it is now the working yarn.

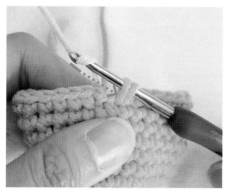

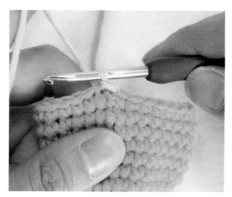

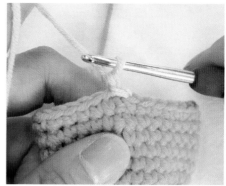

④ Wrap the new yarn over the hook and pull it through the remaining two loops on the hook to complete the stitch.

⑤ Slip stitch in the first stitch to join and complete the round.

⑥ Make a raising chain stitch to bring the yarn up to height.

tip

When working over the yarn tails, keep them to the inside, making sure they are not visible from the outside.

[inside]

[outside]

⑦ Instead of knotting the yarn tails together, work over the two strands with the new yarn for about 4 stitches.

⑧ After working another 4 stitches without working over the tails, the old tails can be cut and the tail ends neatened.

⑨ The first round in the new color is complete.

CUTTING THE YARN AND FINISHING OFF

This is the default method for finishing off all crochet pieces, regardless of the stitch used. It is a way to tie off the work to make sure the stitches don't unravel.

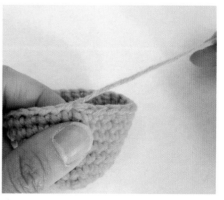

① When you have finished crocheting, without removing the hook, cut the yarn leaving a tail. Wrap the yarn over the hook again.

② Pull the wrapped yarn through the stitch and then pull the yarn tail all the way out, removing the hook.

③ Tug the thread to tighten the knot, then trim the yarn, unless you need the yarn tail to assemble the pieces.

HIDING THE YARN TAILS

This is a way to neaten up the long tails on pieces where the wrong side is visible or not stuffed. In this book.

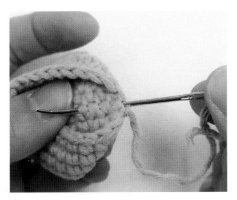

1 Cut the yarn and finish off. Using a yarn needle, sew under a few stitches on the wrong side (inside) of the work to hide the tail.

2 When the tail is neatly sewn in, remove the needle and trim the yarn to finish.

CLOSING THE LAST ROUND

This is used to close the hole after completing the last round. It is needed to finish off the dolls' heads and torsos, so practice it well.

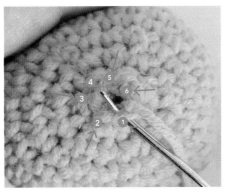

1 After following the instructions for "Cutting the Yarn and Finishing Off", thread the tail onto a yarn needle.

2 Working clockwise, insert the yarn needle (from outside towards center) under the front loop only of each of the six stitches in the last round.

3 Then tug the tail tightly to close the hole.

4 Insert the needle into the center hole, through the stuffing, and bring it out on the other side.

5 Trim the yarn and then using the tweezer, hide the small tail in the stuffed piece.

STUFFING THE DOLL

Some stuffing tends to clump together, so tear off small pieces at a time and fluff it out before inserting it to shape the doll. Take care not to overstuff the doll by adding too much stuffing.

1 Using the forceps, tear off small amounts of stuffing and fill about one-third of the piece.

2 Use your fingers to push the stuffing towards the sides before adding more stuffing. Continue adding more stuffing with the forceps until the desired shape is obtained.

SEWING CROCHET PIECES

Crochet fabrics are more difficult to sew because the surface is more uneven than other fabrics. We'll show you the various ways to sew the different pieces of the doll together.

Straight Stitching	Thread a medium-sized yarn needle with the same type of yarn used to make the doll. To create neat and even sewing stitches, sew in the gaps between the crochet stitches or in the gaps between the crocheted rows or rounds.

1 Embroidery

This stitching is mainly used for decoration. Create even stitches by sewing between each crochet stitch and each row or round.

» Between The Crochet Stitches

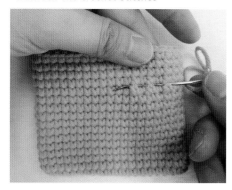

» Between The Rows Or Rounds

2 Whipstitch

This technique leaves the sewing yarn exposed. It is mainly used to attach the arms or ears.

» Across Edges Of Fabric

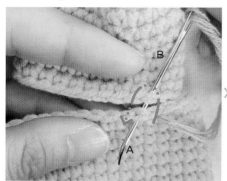 

Bring the needle out from the inside in a stitch on crochet piece A. Insert the needle from front to back in a stitch on crochet piece B and bring it out to the front in a stitch on crochet piece A. Continue sewing in each stitch across, alternating A & B crochet pieces.

» Horizontally Across Stitches - Attaching Arms

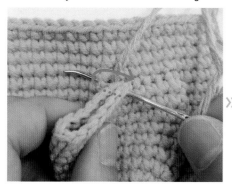 

On the folded piece to be attached, insert the needle under both corresponding stitches, then insert needle in and out between the crochet stiches on the main piece. Continue sewing across until piece is attached.

» Vertically Across Rounds - Attaching Ears

On the folded piece to be attached, insert the needle under both corresponding stitches, then insert needle in and out between crocheted rounds on the main piece. Continue sewing across until piece is attached.

③ Mattress (Invisible) Stitch

The sewing yarn is not visible with this stitch. It connects crochet pieces together firmly and is mainly used to attach the body and head.

① Insert the needle in and out between crochet stiches on first one piece and then on the second piece.

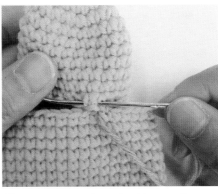

② Now repeat, inserting the needle back in the same place it came out of on each piece.

③ Repeat this for about 3 to 4 stitches.

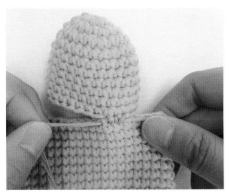

④ Then gently tug the yarn until the stitching disappears.

⑤ Continue doing this until the two pieces are joined together.

Curved Stitching	Separate the yarn used to make the doll into two strands. Thread one strand onto a smaller yarn needle for sewing, hiding the other strand under the piece. This technique is mainly used for stitching on a snout, cheeks, and other curved pieces.

① Using the water-soluble marking pen, mark the position of the curved piece on the fabric, making sure the shape is not distorted.

② With the one strand threaded on the needle, and the other strand tucked under the piece, sew the curved piece onto the fabric, following the marked shape.

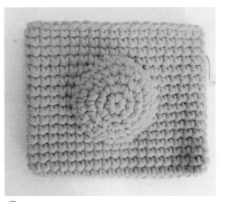

③ The curved piece is attached.

TAKING A BREAK

When you are in the middle of crocheting and need to stop for a while, there is a risk that the stitches will unravel. Here is a tip to prevent that.

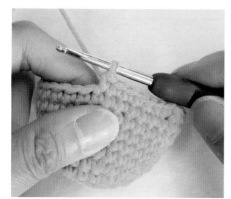

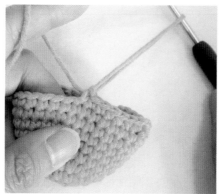

1 When you want to stop, finish the last stitch.

2 Pull the hook to make a large working loop and then remove the hook. Even if the yarn is pulled, the big loop will prevent the stitches from pulling out.

MAKING DOLLS OF DIFFERENT SIZES

By changing the weight of the yarn and the hook size, you can make a variety of different sized dolls using the same pattern.

1 Two strands Medium Weight yarn & 4.00 mm hook

2 Single strand Medium Weight yarn & 3.00 mm hook

3 Single strand Fine Weight yarn & 2.25 mm hook

The photo shows three bears all made with the same pattern, just using different yarns and hooks. The thicker the yarn used (with appropriate hook), the larger the doll, with bigger stitches in the fabric. Please note: When I use one strand of Medium Weight yarn, I use a 3.00 mm hook or US size D-3 (3.25 mm).

◦ Frequently Asked Questions ◦

Q1   **DO YOU NEED SPECIAL YARN TO CROCHET THE DOLLS?**

You can use any type of yarn for making the dolls. The important thing is to use the appropriate hook for the yarn used. (See page 12 - Finding the Correct Hook for the Yarn.) Feel free to choose any type of yarn to create your dolls, regardless of the fiber content. By using a different yarn, you can create a unique doll using the same pattern. But please bear in mind, using pure cotton yarn is more healthier than any other fiber content for babies and children. I used Hello Cotton yarn for the toys in this book.

Q2   **WHY DO CROCHET WORDS CONFUSE ME?**

If you're new to crochet, the terminology can be confusing at first. But if you look at each of the terms, it's easy to understand why they were so named. In the photo, the different crochet terms are labelled on the swatch, so let's make sure you know them before you start making your doll.

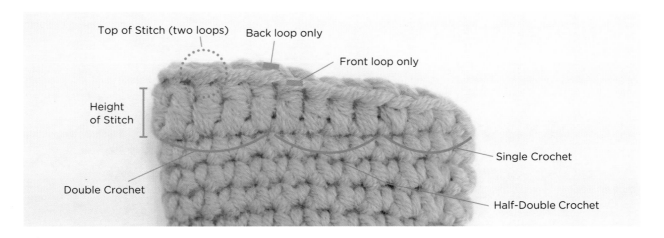

Q3   **DO I HAVE TO JOIN EACH ROUND AND START THE NEXT ROUND WITH CHAIN STITCHES?**

Even if you decide not to join each round, and work the piece in a spiral, you will still be able to follow the pattern, but there will be a difference in how the pieces look. By joining the ends of rounds and starting the next round with raising chain stitches, makes it easier to count the stitches in the round as well as to count the number of rounds worked. It also makes the lines cleaner when you change colors. Compare the photos to see the difference.

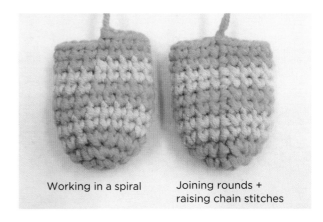

Working in a spiral   Joining rounds + raising chain stitches

Q4   **THE SLIP STITCH JOINS SLANT DIAGONALLY. WHAT SHOULD I DO?**

In crochet, when making a stitch, the right hand naturally pulls to the right (or to the left, if you're left-handed). The stitches made tend to lean towards that direction. To prevent this, pull the wrapped yarn upwards when making a new stitch. This is one way to keep the stitches straight.

◦ **Left:** The joins slant to the right
◦ **Right:** The joins are more straight

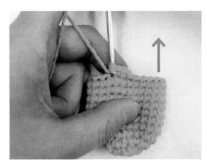

When pulling the wrapped yarn through, consciously pull the yarn upwards. This gives your dolls a neater finish.

Q5 HOW CAN I MAKE MY STITCHES TIGHTER?

For a beautifully made doll, it is important to have all your stitches neat and uniform. Knowing the principles and processes of making crochet stitches, helps to improve your doll-making skills. Let's look at the process of making a single crochet stitch.

» Uneven Stitches

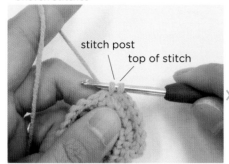

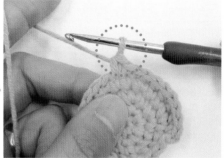

When making a single crochet stitch, the first loop on the hook becomes the post of the stitch, and the second loop becomes the top of the stitch.

Therefore, if the first loop is loose, and the second loop is tight on the hook, the resulting post of the stitch will be slack and create a hole in the fabric.

Similarly, when the first loop is tight and the second loop loose, the stitch post is smaller and the tops of the stitches are floppy.

» How To Crochet Evenly And Tightly

Before starting a single crochet stitch, make sure the loop is tight on the shaft of the hook. Move your index finger in the direction shown, to get tension in the yarn.

After inserting the hook in the stitch on the previous round, tension the yarn again, before wrapping the yarn over the hook.

After pulling the wrapped yarn through the stitch, with the two loops on the hook, tension the yarn once more before completing the stitch. Working like this will make your stitches neat and even.

Q6 HOW DO I DISTINGUISH BETWEEN THE RIGHT AND WRONG SIDES OF THE CROCHET FABRIC?

When working in crocheted rows, the direction changes with each row, so the right and wrong sides alternate. However, when working in rounds, ovals and tubes, the direction stays the same and there is a definite right side and wrong side. In the case of single crochet stitches (✗) which are mostly used in this book, the letter V is visible on the right side of the fabric. On the wrong side, one can see small horizontal lines on the stitches. You can decide which side you want to have on the outside of your doll, and then make sure all your doll pieces have the same side showing.

Single Crochet – right side (outside)   Single Crochet – wrong side (inside)

Q7 HOW DO I WASH MY DOLLS?

Basically, we recommend that you follow the laundry instructions on the yarn label. Use a gentle detergent and rinse very thoroughly. If the yarn allows it, place the doll in a laundry net bag before tumble drying. To dry the stuffing, place the doll in a well-ventilated area.

PROJECTS

ALBERT & BERTHA
the wedding bears

ALBERT | Size (6½" / 17 cm)

YARN: HELLO Cotton Yarn
- Main color (MC) - Mocha (125)
- Color A - Navy Blue (153)
- Color B - Gray-Blue (149)
- Color C - Off-White (155)
- Color D - Light Pink (102)

HOOK: Size B-1 (2.25 mm) – or size suitable for yarn used.

OTHER: Yarn Needle
Embroidery Needle
Toy Stuffing
6 mm Round Black Button x 2 – for Eyes
10 mm Flat Dark Brown Button x 1 – for Nose
Brown Embroidery Thread
6 mm Flat White Button x 2 – for Suspenders

BERTHA | Size (6½" / 17 cm)

YARN: HELLO Cotton Yarn
- Main color (MC) - Mocha (125)
- Color C - Off-White (155)
- Color D - Light Pink (102)

HOOK: Size B-1 (2.25 mm) – or size suitable for yarn used.

OTHER: Yarn Needle
Embroidery Needle
Toy Stuffing
6 mm Round Black Button x 2 – for Eyes
10 mm Flat Dark Brown Button x 1 – for Nose
Brown Embroidery Thread

NOTE

All pieces are made in joined rounds, unless otherwise specified.

SPECIAL STITCHES

Shell: Work 5 double crochet stitches in the same stitch or space specified.

GROOM BEAR

LEGS

First Leg

Round 1: Using Color B, make a Magic Ring; 6 sc in ring. (6 sc)

Round 2: Inc in each st around. (12 sc)

Rounds 3-4: *(2 rounds)* Sc in each st around. (12 sc)

At the end of Round 4, change to Color A.

Rounds 5-7: *(3 rounds)* Sc in each st around. (12 sc)

At the end of Round 7, fasten off.

Second Leg

Rounds 1-7: Repeat Rounds 1-7 of First Leg.

At the end of Round 7, continue with Body. (photo 1)

BODY

Round 8: *(Joining Legs)* Working on Second Leg, sc in each of next 11 sts *(last st remains unworked)*, ch 6; working on First Leg, sc in 2nd st (photo 2), sc in each of next 11 sts; working in ch-6, sc in each of next 6 ch (photo 3); working on Second Leg, sc in next st *(skipped last st)*. (30 sc)

Round 9: Sc in each of next 11 sts (photo 4); working in front loops only of ch-6, sc in each of next 6 ch; sc in each of next 19 sts. (36 sc) (photo 5)

Round 10: [Sc in each of next 5 sts, inc in next st] 6 times. (42 sc)

Rounds 11-14: *(4 Rounds)* Sc in each st around. (42 sc)

At the end of Round 14, change to Color C.

Rounds 15-16: *(2 Rounds)* Sc in each st around. (42 sc)

Round 17: [Sc in each of next 19 sts, dec] 2 times. (40 sc)

Round 18: Sc in each st around. (40 sc)

Round 19: Sc in each of next 9 sts, dec, sc in each of next 18 sts, dec, sc in each of next 9 sts. (38 sc)

Round 20: [Sc in each of next 17 sts, dec] 2 times. (36 sc)

 - Start stuffing, adding more as you go.

Round 21: Sc in each of next 8 sts, dec, sc in each of next 16 sts, dec, sc in each of next 8 sts. (34 sc)

Round 22: [Sc in each of next 15 sts, dec] 2 times. (32 sc)

Round 23: Sc in each of next 7 sts, dec, sc in each of next 14 sts, dec, sc in each of next 7 sts. (30 sc)

Round 24: [Sc in each of next 13 sts, dec] 2 times. (28 sc)

Round 25: Sc in each of next 6 sts, dec, sc in each of next 12 sts, dec, sc in each of next 6 sts. (26 sc)

Round 26: [Sc in each of next 11 sts, dec] 2 times. (24 sc)
Continue stuffing. Fasten off. (photo 6)

HEAD

Round 1: Using MC, make an oval with a foundation chain of 6 stitches; starting in 2nd ch from hook, [sc in each of

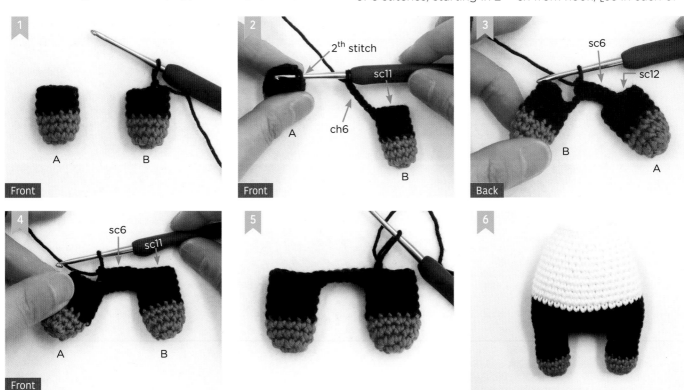

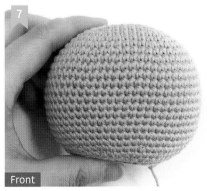

Front

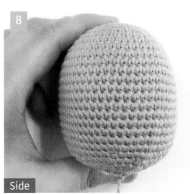

Side

next 4 sts, inc in next st] 2 times. (12 sc)

Round 2: Inc in next st, sc in each of next 3 sts, inc in each of next 3 sts, sc in each of next 3 sts, inc in each of next 2 sts. (18 sc)

Round 3: Sc in next st, inc in next st, sc in each of next 3 sts, [sc in next st, inc in next st] 3 times, sc in each of next 3 sts, [sc in next st, inc in next st] 2 times. (24 sc)

Round 4: Sc in next st, inc in next st, sc in each of next 4 sts, [sc in next st, inc in next st, sc in next st] 3 times, sc in each of next 3 sts, [sc in next st, inc in next st, sc in next st] 2 times. (30 sc)

Round 5: Sc in each of next 3 sts, inc in next st, sc in each of next 3 sts, [sc in each of next 3 sts, inc in next st] 3 times, sc in each of next 3 sts, [sc in each of next 3 sts, inc in next st] 2 times. (36 sc)

Round 6: [Sc in each of next 5 sts, inc in next st] 6 times. (42 sc)

Round 7: Sc in each of next 3 sts, inc in next st, [sc in each of next 6 sts, inc in next st] 5 times, sc in each of next 3 sts. (48 sc)

Round 8: [Sc in each of next 7 sts, inc in next st] 6 times. (54 sc)

Round 9: Sc in each of next 4 sts, inc in next st, [sc in each of next 8 sts, inc in next st] 5 times, sc in each of next 4 sts. (60 sc)

Rounds 10-20: *(11 rounds)* Sc in each st around. (60 sc)

Round 21: Sc in each of next 4 sts, dec, [sc in each of next 8 sts, dec] 5 times, sc in next 4 sts. (54 sc)

  - Start stuffing, adding more as you go.

Round 22: [Sc in each of next 7 sts, dec] 6 times. (48 sc)

Round 23: Sc in each of next 3 sts, dec, [sc in each of next 6 sts, dec] 5 times, sc in next 3 sts. (42 sc)

Round 24: [Sc in each of next 5 sts, dec] 6 times. (36 sc)

Round 25: [Sc in next st, dec] 12 times. (24 sc)

Fasten off, leaving a 20" (50 cm) long tail. *(photos 7 & 8)*

ARM (Make 2)

Round 1: Using MC, make a Magic Ring; 6 sc in ring. (6 sc)

Round 2: [Sc in next st, inc in next st] 3 times. (9 sc)

Rounds 3-4: *(2 rounds)* Sc in each st around. (9 sc)

At the end of Round 4, change to Color C.

Rounds 5-11: *(7 rounds)* Sc in each st around. (9 sc)

Round 12: [Sc in next st, dec] 3 times. (6 sc)

Stuff the Arm about 2/3 full.

Fasten off, leaving a 16" (40 cm) long tail. *(photo 9)*

EAR (Make 2)

Round 1: Using MC, make a Magic Ring; 6 sc in ring. (6 sc)

Round 2: Inc in each st around. (12 sc)

Round 3: [Sc in next st, inc in next st] 6 times. (18 sc)

Rounds 4-5: *(2 rounds)* Sc in each st around. (18 sc)
Fasten off, leaving an 8" (20 cm) long tail. *(photo 10)*

SNOUT

Round 1: Using Color C, make a Magic Ring; 6 sc in ring. (6 sc)

Round 2: Inc in each st around. (12 sc)

Round 3: [Sc in next st, inc in next st] 6 times. (18 sc)

Round 4: Sc in next st, inc in next st, [sc in each of next 2 sts, inc in next st] 5 times, sc in next st. (24 sc)
Fasten off, leaving an 8" (20 cm) long tail.

HAT

Round 1: Using Color A, make a Magic Ring; 6 sc in ring. (6 sc)

Round 2: Inc in each st around. (12 sc)

Round 3: [Sc in next st, inc in next st] 6 times. (18 sc)

Rounds 4-5: *(2 rounds)* Sc in each st around. (18 sc)

At the end of Round 5, change to Color B.

Rounds 6-7: *(2 rounds)* Sc in each st around. (18 sc)

At the end of Round 7, change to Color A.

Round 8: Working in front loops only, [sc in each of next 2 sts, inc in next st] 6 times. (24 sc)
Fasten off, leaving an 8" (20 cm) long tail. (photo 11)

SUSPENDER STRAP (Make 2)

Row 1: Using Color B, ch 29, sc in 5th ch from hook *(skipped ch-4 is buttonhole)*, [sc in next ch] across. (25 sc)

Fasten off, leaving a 6" (15 cm) long tail. (photo 12)

BOWTIE

Row 1: Using Color D, ch 13, sc in 2nd ch from hook, [sc in next ch] across. (12 sc)

Rows 2-5: *(4 rows)* Ch 1, turn, working in **back loops** only, sc in each st across (12 sc)

At the end of Row 5, fasten off, leaving a 12" (30 cm) long tail.

Wrap the long tail around the center of the rows to form a Bowtie shape, leaving the remaining tail for sewing. (photos 13 & 14)

ASSEMBLY (use photos as guide)

Body: Using the long tail sew the Head to Body, making sure a flat side of the head faces to the front.

Arms: Sew the Arms to either side of the Body, one round below the neckline.

Snout: Position the Snout in the center of the face between Rounds 11 & 18, and sew in place.

Ears: Position the Ears on either side of the Head between Rounds 4 & 11, and using long tails, sew in place.

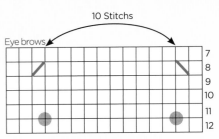

Face:

- Using the Brown thread, sew the Eye Buttons between Rounds 11 & 12 with 10 stitches between them.

- Embroider the Eyebrows above each Eye on Round 8, with 10 stitches between them.

- Using the Brown thread, sew the Nose Button to the top of the Snout.

- Embroider the Mouth on the Snout.

- Using Color D, embroider Cheeks between Rounds 12 & 13 on the outside of each eye.

Accessories:

- Sew each Suspender Strap on either side at the back between Rounds 14 & 15, with 12 stitches between them. Cross the straps at the back and bring to the front.

- On the front, sew the buttons to Round 14, with 12 stitches between them. Fasten the suspenders to the buttons.

- Using the long tail, sew the Bowtie to front of neck.

- Sew the Hat to the top of the Head.

BRIDE BEAR

LEGS

First Leg

Round 1: Using Color C, make a Magic Ring; 6 sc in ring. (6 sc)

Round 2: Inc in each st around. (12 sc)

Rounds 3-4: *(2 rounds)* Sc in each st around. (12 sc)
At the end of Round 4, change to MC.

Rounds 5-7: *(3 rounds)* Sc in each st around. (12 sc)
At the end of Round 7, fasten off.

Second Leg

Rounds 1-7: Repeat Rounds 1-7 of First Leg.

At the end of Round 7, change to Color C and continue with Body. (photo 1)

BODY

Round 8: *(Joining Legs)* Working on Second Leg, sc in each of next 11 sts *(last st remains unworked)*, ch 6; working on First Leg, sc in 2nd st (photo 2), sc in each of next 11 sts; working in ch-6, sc in each of next 6 ch (photo 3); working on Second Leg, sc in next st *(skipped last st)*. (30 sc)

Round 9: Sc in each of next 11 sts (photo 4); working in front loops only of ch-6, sc in each of next 6 ch; sc in each of next 19 sts. (36 sc) (photo 5)

Round 10: [Sc in each of next 5 sts, inc in next st] 6 times. (42 sc)

Rounds 11-14: *(4 Rounds)* Sc in each st around. (42 sc)

Round 15: Working in **back loops** only, sc in each st around. (42 sc0

Round 16: [Sc in each of next 19 sts, dec] 2 times. (40 sc)

Round 17: Sc in each st around. (40 sc)

Round 18: Working in **back loops** only, sc in each of next 9 sts, dec, sc in each of next 18 sts, dec, sc in each of next 9 sts. (38 sc)

Round 19: [Sc in each of next 17 sts, dec] 2 times. (36 sc)
  - Start stuffing, adding more as you go.

Round 20: Sc in each of next 8 sts, dec, sc in each of next 16 sts, dec, sc in each of next 8 sts. (34 sc)

Round 21: [Sc in each of next 15 sts, dec] 2 times. (32 sc)

Round 22: Sc in each of next 7 sts, dec, sc in each of next 14 sts, dec, sc in each of next 7 sts. (30 sc)

Round 23: [Sc in each of next 13 sts, dec] 2 times. (28 sc)

Round 24: Sc in each of next 6 sts, dec, sc in each of next 12 sts, dec, sc in each of next 6 sts. (26 sc)

Round 25: [Sc in each of next 11 sts, dec] 2 times. (24 sc) Continue stuffing. Fasten off. (photo 6)

SKIRT

First Frill

Holding Bride upside down, working in the front loops of Round 14, starting at the back, join Color C to any st. (photo 7)

Round 1: Sc in each st around. (42 sc) (photo 8)

Round 2: [Sc in each of next 13 sts, inc in next st] 3 times. (45 sc)

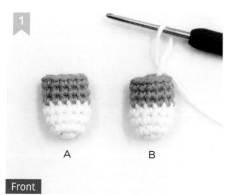
Front — A B

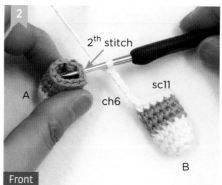

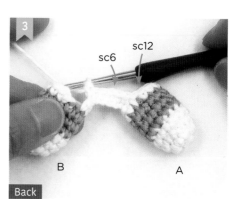
2th stitch — A — ch6 — sc11 — B — Front

sc12 — sc6 — B — A — Back

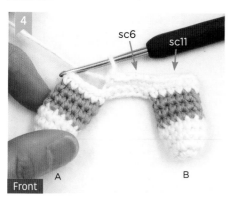

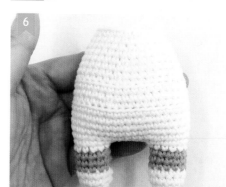
sc6 — sc11 — A — B — Front

Round 3: Sc in each of next 7 sts, inc in next st, [sc in each of next 14 sts, inc in next st] 2 times, sc in each of next 7 sts. (48 sc)

Round 4: [Sc in next st, skip next 2 sts, shell in next st, skip next 2 sts] 8 times. (8 shells)

- Fasten off and weave in ends. (photo 9)

Second Frill

Holding Bride upside down, working in the front loops of Round 17, starting at the back, join Color C to any st. (photo 10)

Round 1: Sc in each st around. (40 sc)

Round 2: [Sc in each of next 19 sts, inc in next st] 2 times. (42 sc)

Round 3: Sc in each st around. (42 sc)

Round 4: [Sc in next st, skip next 2 sts, shell in next st, skip next 2 sts] 7 times. (7 shells)

- Fasten off and weave in ends. (photo 11)

HEAD

Round 1: Using MC, make an oval with a foundation chain of 6 stitches; starting in 2nd ch from hook, [sc in each of next 4 sts, inc in next st] 2 times. (12 sc)

Round 2: Inc in next st, sc in each of next 3 sts, inc in each of next 3 sts, sc in each of next 3 sts, inc in each of next 2 sts. (18 sc)

Round 3: Sc in next st, inc in next st, sc in each of next 3 sts, [sc in next st, inc in next st] 3 times, sc in each of next 3 sts, [sc in next st, inc in next st] 2 times. (24 sc)

Round 4: Sc in next st, inc in next st, sc in each of next 4 sts, [sc in next st, inc in next st, sc in next st] 3 times, sc in each of next 3 sts, [sc in next st, inc in next st, sc in next st] 2 times. (30 sc)

Round 5: Sc in each of next 3 sts, inc in next st, sc in each of next 3 sts, [sc in each of next 3 sts, inc in next st] 3 times, sc in each of next 3 sts, [sc in each of next 3 sts, inc in next st] 2 times. (36 sc)

Round 6: [Sc in each of next 5 sts, inc in next st] 6 times. (42 sc)

Round 7: Sc in each of next 3 sts, inc in next st, [sc in each of next 6 sts, inc in next st] 5 times, sc in each of next 3 sts. (48 sc)

Round 8: [Sc in each of next 7 sts, inc in next st] 6 times. (54 sc)

Round 9: Sc in each of next 4 sts, inc in next st, [sc in each of next 8 sts, inc in next st] 5 times, sc in each of next 4 sts. (60 sc)

Rounds 10-20: (11 rounds) Sc in each st around. (60 sc)

Round 21: Sc in each of next 4 sts, dec, [sc in each of next 8 sts, dec] 5 times, sc in next 4 sts. (54 sc)

- Start stuffing, adding more as you go.

Round 22: [Sc in each of next 7 sts, dec] 6 times. (48 sc)

Round 23: Sc in each of next 3 sts, dec, [sc in each of next 6 sts, dec] 5 times, sc in next 3 sts. (42 sc)

Round 24: [Sc in each of next 5 sts, dec] 6 times. (36 sc)

Round 25: [Sc in next st, dec] 12 times. (24 sc)
Fasten off, leaving a 20" (50 cm) long tail.
(photos 12 & 13)

ARM (Make 2)

Round 1: Using MC, make a Magic Ring; 6 sc in ring. (6 sc)

Round 2: [Sc in next st, inc in next st] 3 times. (9 sc)

Rounds 3-7: *(5 rounds)* Sc in each st around. (9 sc)

At the end of Round 7, change to Color C.

Rounds 8-11: *(4 rounds)* Sc in each st around. (9 sc)

Round 12: [Sc in next st, dec] 3 times. (6 sc)

 - Stuff the Arm about ⅔ full.

Fasten off, leaving a 16" (40 cm) long tail. (photo 14)

EAR (Make 2)

Round 1: Using MC, make a Magic Ring; 6 sc in ring. (6 sc)

Round 2: Inc in each st around. (12 sc)

Round 3: [Sc in next st, inc in next st] 6 times. (18 sc)

Rounds 4-5: *(2 rounds)* Sc in each st around. (18 sc)
Fasten off, leaving an 8" (20 cm) long tail. (photo 15)

SNOUT

Round 1: Using Color C, make a Magic Ring; 6 sc in ring. (6 sc)

Round 2: Inc in each st around. (12 sc)

Round 3: [Sc in next st, inc in next st] 6 times. (18 sc)

Round 4: Sc in next st, inc in next st, [sc in each of next 2 sts, inc in next st] 5 times, sc in next st. (24 sc)

Fasten off, leaving an 8" (20 cm) long tail.

RIBBON

Row 1: Using Color D, ch 17, sc in 2nd ch from hook, [sc in next ch] across. (16 sc)

Rows 2-7: *(6 rows)* Ch 1, turn, working in **back loops** only, sc in each st across (16 sc)

At the end of Row 7, fasten off, leaving a 12" (30 cm) long tail.

Wrap the long tail around the center of the rows to form a Ribbon shape, leaving the remaining tail for sewing. (photos 16 & 17)

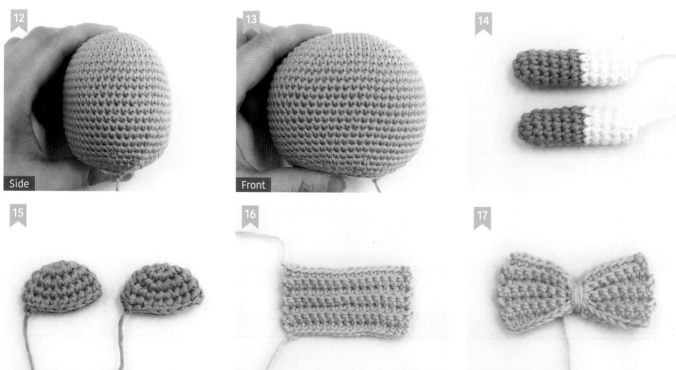

44

ASSEMBLY (use photos as guide)

Body: Using long tail, sew the Head to Body, making sure a flat side of the head faces to the front

Arms: Sew the Arms to either side of the Body, one round below the neckline.

Ears: Position the Ears on either side of the Head between Rounds 4 & 11, and using long tails, sew in place.

Snout: Position the Snout to the center of the face between Rounds 11 & 18, and sew in place.

Face:

- Using the Brown thread, sew the Eye Buttons between Rounds 11 & 12 with 10 stitches between them.

- Embroider the Eyelashes as shown in the diagram.

- Embroider the Eyebrows above each Eye on Round 7, with 10 stitches between them.

- Using the Brown thread, sew the Nose Button to the top of the Snout.

-Embroider the Mouth on the Snout.

- Using Color D, embroider Cheeks between Rounds 12 & 13 on the outside of each eye.

 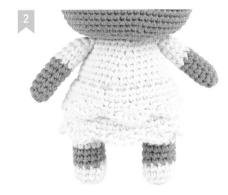

Accessories:

- Using the long tail, sew the Ribbon to the top of Head.

- Using Color D, starting at the front, embroider stitches around the Body between Rounds 17 & 18, tying the ends in a bow.

SAM & PAM
the twins

| **SAM** | Size (8¼" / 21 cm) | **PAM** | Size (8¼" / 21 cm) |

YARN: HELLO Cotton Yarn

    Main color (MC) - Pale Pink (161)

    Color A - Chocolate Brown (168)

    Color B - Purple (143)

    Color C - Chartreuse (130)

    Color D - Lilac (139)

    Color E - Light Yellow (122)

HOOK: Size B-1 (2.25 mm) – or size suitable for yarn used.

OTHER: Yarn Needle

    Embroidery Needle

    Toy Stuffing

    6 mm Flat Wooden Button x 2 – for Suspenders

    Pink Embroidery Thread

YARN: HELLO Cotton Yarn

    Main color (MC) - Pale Pink (161)

    Color A - Chocolate Brown (168)

    Color B - Purple (143)

    Color C - Chartreuse (130)

    Color D - Lilac (139)

    Color E - Light Yellow (122)

HOOK: Size B-1 (2.25 mm) – or size suitable for yarn used.

OTHER: Yarn Needle

    Embroidery Needle

    Toy Stuffing

    6 mm Flat Wooden Button x 2 – for Dress

    Pink Embroidery Thread

NOTE

All pieces are made in joined rounds, unless otherwise specified.

SPECIAL STITCHES

Shell: Work 5 double crochet stitches in the same stitch or space specified.

BOY TWIN

LEGS

First Leg

Round 1: Using Color D, make a Magic Ring; 6 sc in ring. (6 sc)

Round 2: Inc in each st around. (12 sc)

Round 3: [Sc in each of next 2 sts, inc in next st] 4 times. (16 sc)

Round 4: [Sc in each of next 3 sts, inc in next st] 4 times. (20 sc)

Rounds 5-7: *(3 rounds)* Sc in each st around. (20 sc)

At the end of Round 7, change to Color B.

Rounds 8-15: *(8 rounds)* Sc in each st around. (20 sc)

At the end of Round 15, fasten off.

Stuff the Leg.

Second Leg

Rounds 1-15: Repeat Rounds 1-15 of First Leg.

Stuff the Leg.

At the end of Round 15, continue with Body. (photo 1)

BODY

Round 16: *(Joining Legs)* Working on Second Leg, sc in each of next 19 sts *(last st remains unworked)*, ch 10; working on First Leg, sc in 2nd st (photo 2), sc in each of next 19 sts; working in ch-10, sc in each of next 10 ch (photo 3); working on Second Leg, sc in next st *(skipped last st)*. (50 sc)

Round 17: Sc in each of next 19 sts (photo 4); working in front loops only of ch-10, sc in each of next 10 ch; sc in each of next 31 sts. (60 sc) (photo 5)

Rounds 18-23: *(6 Rounds)* Sc in each st around. (60 sc)

At the end of Round 23, change to Color C.

Rounds 24-41: *(18 Rounds - alternating Colors C, D & E every 3 rounds)* Sc in each st around. (60 sc)

At the end of Round 41, change to MC.

Rounds 42-51: *(10 Rounds)* Sc in each st around. (60 sc)

Round 52: Sc in each of next 14 sts, dec, sc in each of next 28 sts, dec, sc in each of next 14 sts. (58 sc)

Round 53: [Sc in each of next 27 sts, dec] 2 times. (56 sc)

Round 54: Sc in each of next 13 sts, dec, sc in each of next 26 sts, dec, sc in each of next 13 sts. (54 sc)

Round 55: [Sc in each of next 25 sts, dec] 2 times. (52 sc)

Round 56: Sc in each of next 12 sts, dec, sc in each of next 24 sts, dec, sc in each of next 12 sts. (50 sc)

Round 57: [Sc in each of next 23 sts, dec] 2 times. (48 sc)

Start stuffing, adding more as you go.

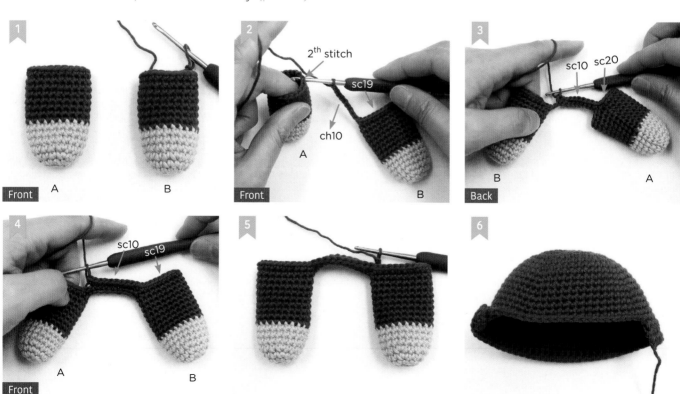

48

Round 58: Sc in each of next 3 sts, dec, [sc in each of next 6 sts, dec] 5 times, sc in each of next 3 sts. (42 sts)

Round 59: [Sc in each of next 5 sts, dec] 6 times. (36 sc)

Round 60: Sc in each of next 2 sts, dec, [sc in each of next 4 sts, dec] 5 times, sc in each of next 2 sts. (30 sts)

Round 61: [Sc in each of next 3 sts, dec] 6 times. (24 sc)

Round 62: Sc in next st, dec, [sc in each of next 2 sts, dec] 5 times, sc in next st. (18 sts)

Round 63: [Sc in next st, dec] 6 times. (12 sc)

Finish stuffing.

Close the last round with a needle. Secure and weave in the end.

HAIR

Round 1: Using Color A, make a Magic Ring; 6 sc in ring. (6 sc)

Round 2: Inc in each st around. (12 sc)

Round 3: [Sc in next st, inc in next st] 6 times. (18 sc)

Round 4: Sc in next st, inc in next st, [sc in each of next 2 sts, inc in next st] 5 times, sc in next st. (24 sc)

Round 5: [Sc in each of next 3 sts, inc in next st] 6 times. (30 sc)

Round 6: Sc in each of next 2 sts, inc in next st, [sc in each of next 4 sts, inc in next st] 5 times, sc in each of next 2 sts. (36 sc)

Round 7: [Sc in each of next 5 sts, inc in next st] 6 times. (42 sc)

Round 8: Sc in each of next 3 sts, inc in next st, [sc in each of next 6 sts, inc in next st] 5 times, sc in each of next 3 sts. (48 sc)

Round 9: [Sc in each of next 23 sts, inc in next st] 2 times. (50 sc)

Round 10: Sc in each of next 12 sts, inc in next st, sc in each of next 24 sts, inc in next st, sc in each of next 12 sts. (52 sc)

Round 11: [Sc in each of next 25 sts, inc in next st] 2 times. (54 sc)

Round 12: Sc in each of next 13 sts, inc in next st, sc in each of next 26 sts, inc in next st, sc in each of next 13 sts. (56 sc)

Round 13: [Sc in each of next 27 sts, inc in next st] 2 times. (58 sc)

Round 14: Sc in each of next 14 sts, inc in next st, sc in each of next 28 sts, inc in next st, sc in each of next 14 sts. (60 sc)

Rounds 15-17: *(3 rounds)* Sc in each st around. (60 sc)

Work continues in Rows.

Row 18: Ch 1, sc in each of next 42 sts. Leave remaining sts unworked.

Rows 19-21: *(3 rows)* Ch 1, turn, sc in each of next 42 sts.

At the end of Row 21, fasten off, leaving a 20" (50 cm) long tail. (photo 6)

ARM (Make 2)

Round 1: Using MC, make a Magic Ring; 6 sc in ring. (6 sc)

Round 2: Inc in each st around. (12 sc)

Round 3: [Sc in each of next 5 sts, inc in next st] 2 times. (14 sc)

Rounds 4-6: *(3 rounds)* Sc in each st around. (14 sc)

At the end of Round 6, change to Color E.

Rounds 7-18: *(12 Rounds - alternating Colors E, D & C every 3 rounds)* Sc in each st around. (14 sc)

Stuff the Arm about ⅔ full.

At the end of Round 18, fasten off, leaving a 16" (40 cm) long tail. (photo 7)

SUSPENDER STRAP (Make 2)

Row 1: Using Color B, ch 50, sc in 6ᵗʰ ch from hook *(skipped ch-5 is buttonhole)*, [sc in next ch] across. (45 sc)

Fasten off, leaving a 6" (15 cm) long tail. (photo 8)

HAT

Round 1: Using Color B, make a Magic Ring; 6 sc in ring. (6 sc)

Round 2: Inc in each st around. (12 sc)

Rounds 3-4: *(2 rounds)* Sc in each st around. (12 sc)

Round 5: [Dec] 6 times (6 sc)

For the following rounds, alternate Colors E, D & C every round.

Round 6: [Sc in next st, inc in next st] 3 times. (9 sc)

Round 7: Sc in next st, inc in next st, [sc in each of next 2 sts, inc in next st] 2 times, sc in next st. (12 sc)

Round 8: [Sc in each of next 3 sts, inc in next st] 3 times. (15 sc)

Round 9: Sc in each of next 2 sts, inc in next st, [sc in each of next 4 sts, inc in next st] 2 times, sc in each of next 2 sts. (18 sc)

Round 10: [Sc in each of next 5 sts, inc in next st] 3 times. (21 sc)

Round 11: Sc in each of next 3 sts, inc in next st, [sc in each of next 6 sts, inc in next st] 2 times, sc in each of next 3 sts. (24 sc)

Round 12: [Sc in each of next 7 sts, inc in next st] 3 times. (27 sc)

Round 13: Sc in each of next 4 sts, inc in next st, [sc in each of next 8 sts, inc in next st] 2 times, sc in each of next 4 sts. (30 sc)

Round 14: [Sc in each of next 9 sts, inc in next st] 3 times. (33 sc)

Change to Color B.

Round 15: Sc in each of next 5 sts, inc in next st, [sc in each of next 10 sts, inc in next st] 2 times, sc in each of next 5 sts. (36 sc)

Round 16: [Sc in each of next 11 sts, inc in next st] 3 times. (39 sc)

Fasten off, leaving a 20" (50 cm) long tail. (photo 9)

ASSEMBLY (use photos as guide)

Hair: Position the Hair on the Head with the front bangs 9 rounds above the neckline. Using the long tails, sew in place.

Arms: Flatten the top of the Arms and sew to either side of the Body between Rounds 40 & 41.

Face:

- Using MC, embroider the Nose between Rounds 45 & 46.

- Using Color A, embroider the Eyes between Rounds 46 & 47, with 10 stitches between them.

- Using Color A, embroider the Mouth on Round 44.

- With Pink, embroider Cheeks between Rounds 44 & 45 on the outside of each eye.

Accessories:

- Sew each Suspender Strap on either side at the back between Rounds 23 & 24, with 17 stitches between them. Cross the straps at the back and bring to the front.

- On the front, sew the buttons to Round 23, with 16 stitches between them. Fasten the Suspenders to the buttons.

- Sew the Hat to the top of the Head at an angle.

LEGS

First Leg

Round 1: Using Color B, make a Magic Ring; 6 sc in ring. (6 sc)

Round 2: Inc in each st around. (12 sc)

Round 3: [Sc in each of next 2 sts, inc in next st] 4 times. (16 sc)

Round 4: [Sc in each of next 3 sts, inc in next st] 4 times. (20 sc)

Rounds 5-7: *(3 rounds)* Sc in each st around. (20 sc)

At the end of Round 7, change to Color MC

Rounds 8-15: *(8 rounds)* Sc in each st around. (20 sc)

At the end of Round 15, fasten off.

Stuff the Leg.

Second Leg

Rounds 1-15: Repeat Rounds 1-15 of First Leg.

Stuff the Leg.

At the end of Round 15, change to Color D and continue with Body. (photo 1)

BODY

Round 16: *(Joining Legs)* Working on Second Leg, sc in each of next 19 sts *(last st remains unworked)*, ch 10; working on First Leg, sc in 2nd st (photo 2), sc in each of next 19 sts; working in ch-10, sc in each of next 10 ch (photo 3); working on Second Leg, sc in next st *(skipped last st)*. (50 sc)

Round 17: Sc in each of next 19 sts (photo 4); working in front loops only of ch-10, sc in each of next 10 ch; sc in each of next 31 sts. (60 sc) (photo 5)

Rounds 18-26: *(9 Rounds)* Sc in each st around. (60 sc)

At the end of Round 26, change to Color B.

Rounds 27-28: *(2 Rounds)* Sc in each st around. (60 sc)

Round 29: Working in **back loops** only, sc in each st around. (60 sc)

Rounds 30-41: *(12 Rounds)* Sc in each st around. (60 sc)

At the end of Round 41, change to MC.

Rounds 42-51: *(10 Rounds)* Sc in each st around. (60 sc)

Round 52: Sc in each of next 14 sts, dec, sc in each of next 28 sts, dec, sc in each of next 14 sts. (58 sc)

Round 53: [Sc in each of next 27 sts, dec] 2 times. (56 sc)

Round 54: Sc in each of next 13 sts, dec, sc in each of next 26 sts, dec, sc in each of next 13 sts. (54 sc)

Round 55: [Sc in each of next 25 sts, dec] 2 times. (52 sc)

Round 56: Sc in each of next 12 sts, dec, sc in each of next 24 sts, dec, sc in each of next 12 sts. (50 sc)

Round 57: [Sc in each of next 23 sts, dec] 2 times. (48 sc)

Start stuffing, adding more as you go.

Round 58: Sc in each of next 3 sts, dec, [sc in each of next 6 sts, dec] 5 times, sc in each of next 3 sts. (42 sts)

Round 59: [Sc in each of next 5 sts, dec] 6 times. (36 sc)

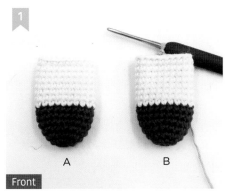

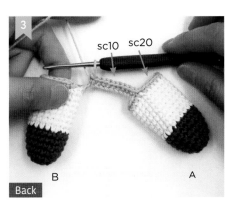

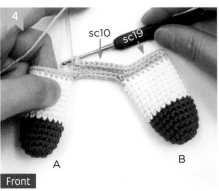

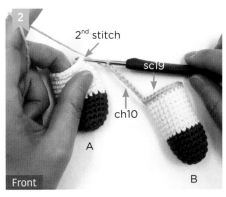

Round 60: Sc in each of next 2 sts, dec, [sc in each of next 4 sts, dec] 5 times, sc in each of next 2 sts. (30 sts)

Round 61: [Sc in each of next 3 sts, dec] 6 times. (24 sc)

Round 62: Sc in next st, dec, [sc in each of next 2 sts, dec] 5 times, sc in next st. (18 sts)

Round 63: [Sc in next st, dec] 6 times. (12 sc)

Finish stuffing.

Close the last round with a needle. Secure and weave in the end.

SKIRT

Holding Girl Twin upside down, working in the front loops of Round 28, starting at the back, join Color E to any st. (photo 6)

For the following rounds, alternate Colors E, D & C every 2 rounds.

Round 1: Sc in each st around. (60 sc) (photo 7)

Round 2: [Sc in each of next 19 sts, inc in next st] 3 times. (63 sc)

Round 3: Sc in each of next 10 sts, inc in next st, [sc in each of next 20 sts, inc in next st] 2 times, sc in each of next 10 sts. (66 sts)

Round 4: [Sc in each of next 21 sts, inc in next st] 3 times. (69 sc)

Round 5: Sc in each of next 11 sts, inc in next st, [sc in each of next 22 sts, inc in next st] 2 times, sc in each of next 11 sts. (72 sts)

Round 6: [Sc in each of next 23 sts, inc in next st] 3 times. (75 sc)

Round 7: Sc in each of next 12 sts, inc in next st, [sc in each of next 24 sts, inc in next st] 2 times, sc in each of next 12 sts. (78 sts)

Round 8: [Sc in each of next 25 sts, inc in next st] 3 times. (81 sc)

Round 9: Sc in each of next 13 sts, inc in next st, [sc in each of next 26 sts, inc in next st] 2 times, sc in each of next 13 sts. (84 sts)

Round 10: [Sc in each of next 27 sts, inc in next st] 3 times. (87 sc)

Round 11: Sc in each of next 14 sts, inc in next st, [sc in each of next 28 sts, inc in next st] 2 times, sc in each of next 14 sts. (90 sts)

Round 12: [Sc in each of next 29 sts, inc in next st] 3 times. (93 sc)

Fasten off and weave in ends. (photo 8)

ARM (Make 2)

Round 1: Using MC, make a Magic Ring; 6 sc in ring. (6 sc)

Round 2: Inc in each st around. (12 sc)

Round 3: [Sc in each of next 5 sts, inc in next st] 2 times. (14 sc)

Rounds 4-6: *(3 rounds)* Sc in each st around. (14 sc)

At the end of Round 6, change to Color B.

Rounds 7-12: *(6 Rounds)* Sc in each st around. (14 sc)

Rounds 13-18: *(6 Rounds - alternating Colors D, E & C every 2 rounds)* Sc in each st around. (14 sc)

Stuff the Arm about ⅔ full.

At the end of Round 18, fasten off, leaving a 16" (40 cm) long tail. (photo 9)

HAIR

Round 1: Using Color A, make a Magic Ring; 6 sc in ring. (6 sc)

Round 2: Inc in each st around. (12 sc)

Round 3: [Sc in next st, inc in next st] 6 times. (18 sc)

Round 4: Sc in next st, inc in next st, [sc in each of next 2 sts, inc in next st] 5 times, sc in next st. (24 sc)

Round 5: [Sc in each of next 3 sts, inc in next st] 6 times. (30 sc)

Round 6: Sc in each of next 2 sts, inc in next st, [sc in each of next 4 sts, inc in next st] 5 times, sc in each of next 2 sts. (36 sc)

Round 7: [Sc in each of next 5 sts, inc in next st] 6 times. (42 sc)

Round 8: Sc in each of next 3 sts, inc in next st, [sc in each of next 6 sts, inc in next st] 5 times, sc in each of next 3 sts. (48 sc)

Round 9: [Sc in each of next 23 sts, inc in next st] 2 times. (50 sc)

Round 10: Sc in each of next 12 sts, inc in next st, sc in each of next 24 sts, inc in next st, sc in each of next 12 sts. (52 sc)

Round 11: [Sc in each of next 25 sts, inc in next st] 2 times. (54 sc)

Round 12: Sc in each of next 13 sts, inc in next st, sc in each of next 26 sts, inc in next st, sc in each of next 13 sts. (56 sc)

Round 13: [Sc in each of next 27 sts, inc in next st] 2 times. (58 sc)

Round 14: Sc in each of next 14 sts, inc in next st, sc in each of next 28 sts, inc in next st, sc in each of next 14 sts. (60 sc)

Rounds 15-17: *(3 rounds)* Sc in each st around. (60 sc)

Round 18: [Sc in next st, skip next 2 sts, shell in next st, skip next 2 sts] 10 times. (10 shells)

Fasten off, leaving a 20" (50 cm) long tail. (photo 10)

Hair Buns (Make 2)

Round 1: Using Color A, make a Magic Ring; 6 sc in ring. (6 sc)

Round 2: Inc in each st around. (12 sc)

Rounds 3-5: *(3 rounds)* Sc in each st around. (12 sc)

Round 6: [Dec] 6 times. (6 sc)

Round 7: Working in **front loops** only, inc in each st around. (12 sc)

Round 8: [Sc in next st, inc in next st] 6 times. (18 sc)

Rounds 9-11: *(3 rounds)* Sc in each st around. (18 sc)

Round 12: [Sc in next st, dec] 6 times. (12 sc)

Round 13: [Dec] 6 times. (6 sc)

Fasten off, leaving a 20" (50 cm) long tail. *(photo 11)*

RIBBON (Make 2 - 1 in Color C & 1 in Color E)

Row 1: Ch 13, sc in 2nd ch from hook, [sc in next ch] across. (12 sc)

Rows 2-5: *(4 rows)* Ch 1, turn, working in **back loops** only, sc in each st across (12 sc)

At the end of Row 5, fasten off, leaving a 12" (30 cm) long tail.

Wrap the long tail around the center of the rows to form a Ribbon shape, leaving the remaining tail for sewing. *(photos 12 & 13)*

53

ASSEMBLY (use photos as guide)

Hair:

- Position the Hair on the Head with the front bangs 9 rounds above the neckline. Using the long tails, sew in place.

- Position the Hair buns symmetrically on either side of the Hair at Round 8, and secure in place.

Face

- Using MC, embroider the Nose between Rounds 45 &46.

- Using Color A, embroider the Eyes between Rounds 46 & 47, with 10 stitches between them.

- Using Color A, embroider the Mouth on Round 44.

- With Pink, embroider Cheeks between Rounds 44 & 45 on the outside of each eye.

Arms:

- Flatten the top of the Arms and sew to either side of the Body between Rounds 40 & 41.

Accessories:

- Sew buttons to the front of the Dress.

- Sew the Ribbons to the front of each Hair Bun

LOGAN & LAURA
the young couple

LOGAN | Size (9½" / 24 cm)

YARN: HELLO Cotton Yarn
- Main color (MC) - Pale Pink (161)
- Color A - Copper Brown (166)
- Color B - Lime Green (131)
- Color C - Cream (156)
- Color D - Mocha (125)
- Color E - Chocolate Brown (168)
- Color F - Gray-Blue (149)

HOOK: Size B-1 (2.25 mm) - or size suitable for yarn used

OTHER: Yarn Needle
Embroidery Needle
Toy Stuffing
5 mm Round Black Button x 2 - for Eyes
10 mm Flat Red Button x 2 - for Suspenders
Pink Embroidery Thread
Beige Felt - for Knee Patches

LAURA | Size (9½" / 24 cm)

YARN: HELLO Cotton Yarn
- Main color (MC) - Pale Pink (161)
- Color A - Copper Brown (166)
- Color B - Lime Green (131)
- Color C - Cream (156)
- Color D - Mocha (125)
- Color G - Kelly Green (132)

HOOK: Size B-1 (2.25 mm) - or size suitable for yarn used

OTHER: Yarn Needle
Embroidery Needle
Toy Stuffing
5 mm Round Black Button x 2 - for Eyes
6 mm Flat Red Button x 2 - for Shoes
Pink Embroidery Thread
Checked Fabric:
17⅔" (45 cm) by 2" (5 cm) - for Skirt
13⅔" (35 cm) by 2⅔" (7 cm) - for Scarf

All pieces are made in joined rounds, unless otherwise specified.

SPECIAL STITCHES

Shell: Work 5 double crochet stitches in the same stitch or space specified.

YOUNG BOY

LEGS

First Leg

Round 1: Using Color D, make a Magic Ring; 6 sc in ring. (6 sc)

Round 2: Inc in each st around. (12 sc)

Round 3: [Sc in next st, inc in next st] 6 times. (18 sc)

Round 4: Sc in each of next 6 sts, [inc] 6 times, sc in each of next 6 sts. (24 sc)

Round 5: Sc in each of next 6 sts, [sc in next st, inc in next st] 6 times, sc in each of next 6 sts. (30 sc)

Round 6: Working in **back loops** only, sc in each st around. (30 sc)

Change to Color E.

Round 7: Working in **back loops** only, sc in each st around. (30 sc)

Round 8: Sc in each of next 6 sts, [sc in next st, dec] 6 times, sc in each of next 6 sts. (24 sc)

Round 9: Sc in each of next 6 sts, [dec] 6 times, sc in each of next 6 sts. (18 sc)

Round 10: Sc in each of next 5 sts, [dec] 4 times, sc in each of next 4 sts. (14 sc)

Rounds 11-12: *(2 rounds)* Sc in each st around. (14 sc)

At the end of Round 12, change to Color F.

Rounds 13-24: *(12 rounds)* Sc in each st around. (14 sc)

At the end of Round 24, fasten off.

Second Leg

Rounds 1-24: Repeat Rounds 1-24 of First Leg.

At the end of Round 24, continue with Body. *(photo 1)*

BODY

Round 25: *(Joining Legs)* Working on Second Leg, sc in each of next 12 sts *(2 sts remain unworked)*, ch 7; working on First Leg, sc in 5th st *(photo 2)*, sc in each of next 13 sts; working in ch-7, sc in each of next 7 ch *(photo 3)*; working on Second Leg, sc in each of next 2 sts. (35 sc)

Round 26: Sc in each of next 12 sts *(photo 4)*; working in front loops only of ch-7, sc in each of next 7 ch; sc in each of next 23 sts. (42 sc) *(photo 5)*

Round 27: Sc in each of next 3 sts, inc in next st, [sc in each of next 6 sts, inc in next st] 5 times, sc in each of next 3 sts. (48 sc)

Rounds 28-32: *(5 Rounds)* Sc in each st around. (48 sc)

For the following rounds, alternate Colors D, C & B every round.

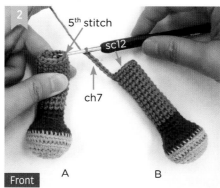

Front   A   B   5th stitch   sc12   ch7

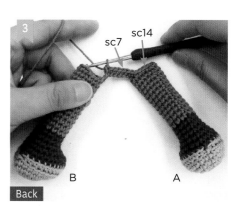

Back   B   A   sc7   sc14

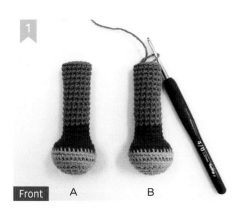

Front   A   B   sc7   sc12

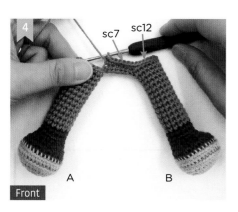

Front   A   B

Rounds 33-35: *(3 Rounds)* Sc in each st around. (48 sc)

Round 36: Sc in each of next 7 sts, dec, [sc in each of next 14 sts, dec] 2 times, sc in each of next 7 sts. (45 sc)

Rounds 37-38: *(2 Rounds)* Sc in each st around. (45 sc)

Start stuffing, adding more as you go.

Round 39: [Sc in each of next 13 sts, dec] 3 times. (42 sc)

Round 40: Sc in each st around. (42 sc)

Round 41: Sc in each of next 6 sts, dec, [sc in each of next 12 sts, dec] 2 times, sc in each of next 6 sts. (39 sc)

Round 42: Sc in each st around. (39 sc)

Round 43: [Sc in each of next 11 sts, dec] 3 times. (36 sc)

Round 44: Sc in each st around. (36 sc)

Round 45: Sc in each of next 5 sts, dec, [sc in each of next 10 sts, dec] 2 times, sc in each of next 5 sts. (33 sc)

Round 46: Sc in each st around. (33 sc)

Round 47: [Sc in each of next 9 sts, dec] 3 times. (30 sc)

Round 48: Sc in each of next 4 sts, dec, [sc in each of next 8 sts, dec] 2 times, sc in each of next 4 sts. (27 sc)

Round 49: [Sc in each of next 7 sts, dec] 3 times. (24 sc)

Continue stuffing. Fasten off. (photo 6)

HEAD

Round 1: Using MC, make a Magic Ring; 6 sc in ring. (6 sc)

Round 2: Inc in each st around. (12 sc)

Round 3: [Sc in next st, inc in next st] 6 times. (18 sc)

Round 4: Sc in next st, inc in next st, [sc in each of next 2 sts, inc in next st] 5 times, sc in next st. (24 sc)

Round 5: [Sc in each of next 3 sts, inc in next st] 6 times. (30 sc)

Round 6: Sc in each of next 2 sts, inc in next st, [sc in each of next 4 sts, inc in next st] 5 times, sc in each of next 2 sts. (36 sc)

Round 7: [Sc in each of next 5 sts, inc in next st] 6 times. (42 sc)

Round 8: Sc in each of next 3 sts, inc in next st, [sc in each of next 6 sts, inc in next st] 5 times, sc in each of next 3 sts. (48 sc)

Round 9: [Sc in each of next 7 sts, inc in next st] 6 times. (54 sc)

Round 10: Sc in each of next 4 sts, inc in next st, [sc in each of next 8 sts, inc in next st] 5 times, sc in each of next 4 sts. (60 sc)

Rounds 11-20: *(10 rounds)* Sc in each st around. (60 sc)

Round 21: Sc in each of next 4 sts, dec, [sc in each of next 8 sts, dec] 5 times, sc in next 4 sts. (54 sc)

Start stuffing, adding more as you go.

Round 22: [Sc in each of next 7 sts, dec] 6 times. (48 sc)

Round 23: Sc in each of next 3 sts, dec, [sc in each of next 6 sts, dec] 5 times, sc in next 3 sts. (42 sc)

Round 24: [Sc in each of next 5 sts, dec] 6 times. (36 sc)

Round 25: Sc in each of next 2 sts, dec, [sc in each of next 4 sts, dec] 5 times, sc in next 2 sts. (30 sc)

Round 26: [Sc in each of next 3 sts, dec] 6 times. (24 sc)

Fasten off, leaving a 20" (50 cm) long tail. (photo 7)

ARM (Make 2)

Round 1: Using MC, make a Magic Ring; 6 sc in ring. (6 sc)

Round 2: Inc in each st around. (12 sc)

Rounds 3-4: *(2 rounds)* Sc in each st around. (12 sc)

Round 5: Sc in each of next 5 sts, [(2 dc) in next st] 2 times, sc in each of next 5 sts. (10 sc & 4 dc)

Round 6: Sc in each of next 5 sts, [dec] 2 times, sc in each of next 5 sts. (12 sc)

Round 7: Sc in each of next 4 sts, [dec] 2 times, sc in each of next 4 sts. (10 sc)

For the following rounds, alternate Colors B, C & D every round.

Rounds 8-20: *(13 Rounds)* Sc in each st around. (10 sc)

Stuff the Arm about ⅔ full.

Round 21: [Sc in each of next 3 sts, dec] 2 times. (8 sc)

Fasten off, leaving a 16" (40 cm) long tail. (photo 8)

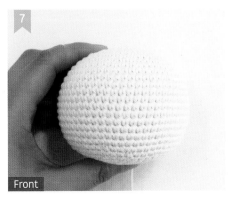

Front

HAIR

Round 1: Using Color A, make a Magic Ring; 6 sc in ring. (6 sc)

Round 2: Inc in each st around. (12 sc)

Round 3: [Sc in next st, inc in next st] 6 times. (18 sc)

Round 4: Sc in next st, inc in next st, [sc in each of next 2 sts, inc in next st] 5 times, sc in next st. (24 sc)

Round 5: [Sc in each of next 3 sts, inc in next st] 6 times. (30 sc)

Round 6: Sc in each of next 2 sts, inc in next st, [sc in each of next 4 sts, inc in next st] 5 times, sc in each of next 2 sts. (36 sc)

Round 7: [Sc in each of next 5 sts, inc in next st] 6 times. (42 sc)

Round 8: Sc in each of next 3 sts, inc in next st, [sc in each of next 6 sts, inc in next st] 5 times, sc in each of next 3 sts. (48 sc)

Round 9: [Sc in each of next 7 sts, inc in next st] 6 times. (54 sc)

Round 10: Sc in each of next 4 sts, inc in next st, [sc in each of next 8 sts, inc in next st] 5 times, sc in each of next 4 sts. (60 sc)

Rounds 11-18: *(8 rounds)* Sc in each st around. (60 sc)

Round 19: Sc in each of next 3 sts, hdc in each of next 4 sts, dc in each of next 8 sts, hdc in each of next 4 sts, sc in each of next 41 sts. (44 sc, 8 hdc & 8 dc)

Work continues in Rows.

Row 20: Ch 1, turn, sc in first st, sc in each of next 37 sts. (38 sc) Leave remaining sts unworked.

Rows 21-23: *(3 rows)* Ch 1, turn, sc in each st across. (38 sc)

Fasten off, leaving a 20" (50 cm) long tail. (photo 9)

HAT

Round 1: Using Color D, make a Magic Ring; 6 sc in ring. (6 sc)

Round 2: Inc in each st around. (12 sc)

Round 3: [Sc in next st, inc in next st] 6 times. (18 sc)

Round 4: Sc in next st, inc in next st, [sc in each of next 2 sts, inc in next st] 5 times, sc in next st. (24 sc)

Round 5: [Sc in each of next 3 sc, inc in next st] 6 times. (30 sc)

Round 6: Sc in each of next 2 sts, inc in next st, [sc in each of next 4 sts, inc in next st] 5 times, sc in each of next 2 sts. (36 sc)

Round 7: [Sc in each of next 5 sc, inc in next st] 6 times. (42 sc)

Round 8: Sc in each of next 3 sts, inc in next st, [sc in each of next 6 sts, inc in next st] 5 times, sc in each of next 3 sts. (48 sc)

Round 9: [Sc in each of next 7 sc, inc in next st] 6 times. (54 sc)

Round 10: Sc in each of next 4 sts, inc in next st, [sc in each of next 8 sts, inc in next st] 5 times, sc in each of next 4 sts. (60 sc)

Rounds 11-16: *(6 rounds)* Sc in each st around. (60 sc)

At the end of Round 16, change to Color F.

Rounds 17-18: *(2 rounds)* Sc in each st around. (60 sc)

At the end of Round 18, change to Color D.

Round 19: Working in front loops only, [sc in each of next 5 sc, inc in next st] 10 times. (70 sc)

Round 20: Sc in each of next 3 sts, inc in next st, [sc in each of next 6 sts, inc in next st] 9 times, sc in each of next 3 sts. (80 sc)

Round 21: [sc in each of next 7 sts, inc in next st] 10 times. (90 sc)

Round 22: Sc in each of next 4 sts, inc in next st, [sc in each of next 8 sts, inc in next st] 9 times, sc in each of next 4 sts. (100 sc)

Fasten off, leaving an 8" (20 cm) long tail. (photo 10)

SUSPENDER STRAP (Make 2)

Row 1: Using Color E, ch 40, sc in 6th ch from hook *(skipped ch-5 is buttonhole)*, [sc in next ch] across. (35 sc)

Fasten off, leaving a 6" (15 cm) long tail. (photo 11)

ASSEMBLY (use photos as guide)

Body: Using the long tail, sew the Head to Body.

Arms: Sew the Arms to either side of the Body, one round below neckline.

Face:

- Using MC, thickly embroider the Nose between the 10th & 11th rounds up from neckline.

- Using Color A, embroider the Eyes between the 11th & 12th rounds up from neckline, with 12 stitches between them.

- Using Pink, embroider the Cheeks between the 10th & 11th rounds up from neckline, one stitch away from the outside of each Eye.

Hair – Position the Hair on the Head, and using the long tail, sew in place.

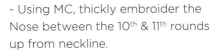

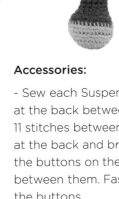

Accessories:

- Sew each Suspender Strap on either side at the back between Rounds 32 & 33, with 11 stitches between them. Cross the straps at the back and bring to the front. Sew the buttons on the front, with 13 stitches between them. Fasten the suspenders to the buttons.

- Sew a Felt Patch on each knee.

- Place the Hat on the Head.

YOUNG GIRL

LEGS

First Leg

Round 1: Using Color D, make a Magic Ring; 6 sc in ring. (6 sc)

Round 2: Inc in each st around. (12 sc)

Round 3: [Sc in next st, inc in next st] 6 times. (18 sc)

Round 4: Sc in each of next 6 sts, [inc] 6 times, sc in each of next 6 sts. (24 sc)

Change to Color G.

Round 5: Working in **back loops** only, sc in each of next 6 sts, [sc in next st, inc in next st] 6 times, sc in each of next 6 sts. (30 sc)

Rounds 6-7: *(2 rounds)* Sc in each st around. (30 sc)

Round 8: Sc in each of next 6 sts, [sc in next st, dec] 6 times, sc in each of next 6 sts. (24 sc)

Change to Color C.

Round 9: Working in **back loops** only, sc in each of next 6 sts, [dec] 6 times, sc in each of next 6 sts. (18 sc)

Round 10: Sc in each of next 5 sts, [dec] 4 times, sc in each of next 4 sts. (14 sc)

Rounds 11-15: *(5 rounds)* Sc in each st around. (14 sc)

At the end of Round 15, change to Color MC.

Rounds 16-22: *(7 rounds)* Sc in each st around. (14 sc)

At the end of Round 22, change to Color C.

Rounds 23-24: *(2 rounds)* Sc in each st around. (14 sc)

At the end of Round 24, fasten off.

Second Leg

Rounds 1-24: Repeat Rounds 1-24 of First Leg.

At the end of Round 24, continue with Body. (photo 1)

BODY

Round 25: *(Joining Legs)* Working on Second Leg, sc in each of next 12 sts *(2 sts remain unworked)*, ch 7; working on First Leg, sc in 5th st (photo 2), sc in each of next 13 sts; working in ch-7, sc in each of next 7 ch (photo 3); working on Second Leg, sc in each of next 2 sts. (35 sc)

Round 26: Sc in each of next 12 sts (photo 4); working in front loops only of ch-7, sc in each of next 7 ch; sc in each of next 23 sts. (42 sc)

Round 27: Sc in each of next 3 sts, inc in next st, [sc in each of next 6 sts, inc in next st] 5 times, sc in each of next 3 sts. (48 sc)

Rounds 28-31: *(4 Rounds)* Sc in each st around. (48 sc)

Change to Color B.

Rounds 32-34: *(3 Rounds)* Sc in each st around. (48 sc)

Round 35: Working in **back loops** only, sc in each of next 7 sts, dec, [sc in each of next 14 sts, dec] 2 times, sc in each of next 7 sts. (45 sc)

Rounds 36-37: *(2 Rounds)* Sc in each st around. (45 sc)

Start stuffing, adding more as you go.

Round 38: [Sc in each of next 13 sts, dec] 3 times. (42 sc)

Change to Color D.

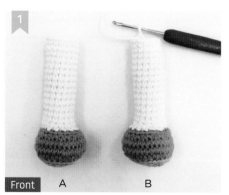

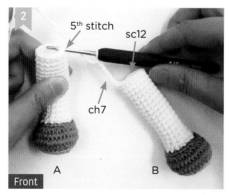

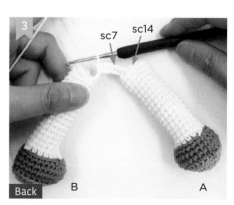

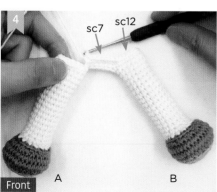

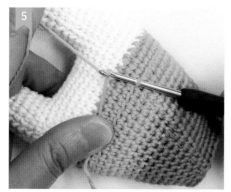

Round 39: Sc in each st around. (42 sc)

Round 40: Sc in each of next 6 sts, dec, [sc in each of next 12 sts, dec] 2 times, sc in each of next 6 sts. (39 sc) Change to Color G.

Round 41: Sc in each st around. (39 sc)

Round 42: [Sc in each of next 11 sts, dec] 3 times. (36 sc)

Round 43: Sc in each st around. (36 sc)

Round 44: Sc in each of next 5 sts, dec, [sc in each of next 10 sts, dec] 2 times, sc in each of next 5 sts. (33 sc)

Round 45: Sc in each st around. (33 sc)

Round 46: [Sc in each of next 9 sts, dec] 3 times. (30 sc)

Round 47: Sc in each of next 4 sts, dec, [sc in each of next 8 sts, dec] 2 times, sc in each of next 4 sts. (27 sc)

Round 48: [Sc in each of next 7 sts, dec] 3 times. (24 sc) Continue stuffing. Fasten off.

Shirt Detail

Holding doll upside down, working in the front loops of Round 34, starting at the back, join Color B to any st. (photo 5)

Round 1: Sc in each st around. (48 sc) (photo 6)

Rounds 2-3: (2 rounds) Sc in each st around. (48 sc)

At the end of Round 3, fasten off, leaving a 16" (40 cm) long tail. (photo 7)

HEAD

Round 1: Using MC, make a Magic Ring; 6 sc in ring. (6 sc)

Round 2: Inc in each st around. (12 sc)

Round 3: [Sc in next st, inc in next st] 6 times. (18 sc)

Round 4: Sc in next st, inc in next st, [sc in each of next 2 sts, inc in next st] 5 times, sc in next st. (24 sc)

Round 5: [Sc in each of next 3 sts, inc in next st] 6 times. (30 sc)

Round 6: Sc in each of next 2 sts, inc in next st, [sc in each of next 4 sts, inc in next st] 5 times, sc in each of next 2 sts. (36 sc)

Round 7: [Sc in each of next 5 sts, inc in next st] 6 times. (42 sc)

Round 8: Sc in each of next 3 sts, inc in next st, [sc in each of next 6 sts, inc in next st] 5 times, sc in each of next 3 sts. (48 sc)

Round 9: [Sc in each of next 7 sts, inc in next st] 6 times. (54 sc)

Round 10: Sc in each of next 4 sts, inc in next st, [sc in each of next 8 sts, inc in next st] 5 times, sc in each of next 4 sts. (60 sc)

Rounds 11-20: (10 rounds) Sc in each st around. (60 sc)

Round 21: Sc in each of next 4 sts, dec, [sc in each of next 8 sts, dec] 5 times, sc in next 4 sts. (54 sc)

Start stuffing, adding more as you go.

Round 22: [Sc in each of next 7 sts, dec] 6 times. (48 sc)

Round 23: Sc in each of next 3 sts, dec, [sc in each of next 6 sts, dec] 5 times, sc in next 3 sts. (42 sc)

Round 24: [Sc in each of next 5 sts, dec] 6 times. (36 sc)

Round 25: Sc in each of next 2 sts, dec, [sc in each of next 4 sts, dec] 5 times, sc in next 2 sts. (30 sc)

Round 26: [Sc in each of next 3 sts, dec] 6 times. (24 sc)

Fasten off, leaving a 20" (50 cm) long tail. (photo 8)

ARM (Make 2)

Round 1: Using MC, make a Magic Ring; 6 sc in ring. (6 sc)

Round 2: Inc in each st around. (12 sc)

Rounds 3-4: (2 rounds) Sc in each st around. (12 sc)

Round 5: Sc in each of next 5 sts, [(2 dc) in next st] 2 times, sc in each of next 5 sts. (10 sc & 4 dc)

Round 6: Sc in each of next 5 sts, [dec] 2 times, sc in each of next 5 sts. (12 sc)

Round 7: Sc in each of next 4 sts, [dec] 2 times, sc in each of next 4 sts. (10 sc)

Change to Color B.

Rounds 8-12: (5 Rounds) Sc in each st around. (10 sc)

Change to Color D.

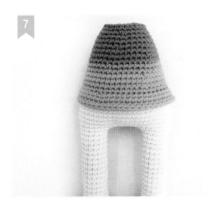

Front

Rounds 13-14: *(2 Rounds)* Sc in each st around. (10 sc)

Change to Color G.

Rounds 15-20: *(6 Rounds)* Sc in each st around. (10 sc) Stuff the Arm about ⅔ full.

Round 21: [Sc in each of next 3 sts, dec] 2 times. (8 sc)

Fasten off, leaving a 16" (40 cm) long tail. (photo 9)

HAIR

Round 1: Using Color A, make a Magic Ring; 6 sc in ring. (6 sc)

Round 2: Inc in each st around. (12 sc)

Round 3: [Sc in next st, inc in next st] 6 times. (18 sc)

Round 4: Sc in next st, inc in next st, [sc in each of next 2 sts, inc in next st] 5 times, sc in next st. (24 sc)

Round 5: [Sc in each of next 3 sts, inc in next st] 6 times. (30 sc)

Round 6: Sc in each of next 2 sts, inc in next st, [sc in each of next 4 sts, inc in next st] 5 times, sc in each of next 2 sts. (36 sc)

Round 7: [Sc in each of next 5 sts, inc in next st] 6 times. (42 sc)

Round 8: Sc in each of next 3 sts, inc in next st, [sc in each of next 6 sts, inc in next st] 5 times, sc in each of next 3 sts. (48 sc)

Round 9: [Sc in each of next 7 sts, inc in next st] 6 times. (54 sc)

Round 10: Sc in each of next 4 sts, inc in next st, [sc in each of next 8 sts, inc in next st] 5 times, sc in each of next 4 sts. (60 sc)

Rounds 11-18: *(8 rounds)* Sc in each st around. (60 sc)

Round 19: [Sc in next st, skip next 2 sts, shell in next st, skip next 2 sts] 10 times. (10 shells)

Fasten off, leaving a 20" (50 cm) long tail.

HAT

Round 1: Using Color D, make a Magic Ring; 6 sc in ring. (6 sc)

Round 2: Inc in each st around. (12 sc)

Round 3: [Sc in next st, inc in next st] 6 times. (18 sc)

Round 4: Sc in next st, inc in next st, [sc in each of next 2 sts, inc in next st] 5 times, sc in next st. (24 sc)

Round 5: [Sc in each of next 3 sc, inc in next st] 6 times. (30 sc)

Round 6: Sc in each of next 2 sts, inc in next st, [sc in each of next 4 sts, inc in next st] 5 times, sc in each of next 2 sts. (36 sc)

Round 7: [Sc in each of next 5 sc, inc in next st] 6 times. (42 sc)

Round 8: Sc in each of next 3 sts, inc in next st, [sc in each of next 6 sts, inc in next st] 5 times, sc in each of next 3 sts. (48 sc)

Round 9: [Sc in each of next 7 sc, inc in next st] 6 times. (54 sc)

Round 10: Sc in each of next 4 sts, inc in next st, [sc in each of next 8 sts, inc in next st] 5 times, sc in each of next 4 sts. (60 sc)

Rounds 11-16: *(6 rounds)* Sc in each st around. (60 sc)

At the end of Round 16, change to Color G.

Rounds 17-18: *(2 rounds)* Sc in each st around. (60 sc)

At the end of Round 18, change to Color D.

Round 19: Working in front loops only, [sc in each of next 5 sc, inc in next st] 10 times. (70 sc)

Round 20: Sc in each of next 3 sts, inc in next st, [sc in each of next 6 sts, inc in next st] 9 times, sc in each of next 3 sts. (80 sc)

Round 21: [sc in each of next 7 sts, inc in next st] 10 times. (90 sc)

Round 22: Sc in each of next 4 sts, inc in next st, [sc in each of next 8 sts, inc in next st] 9 times, sc in each of next 4 sts. (100 sc)

Fasten off, leaving an 8" (20 cm) long tail. (photo 10)

Body: Using long tail, sew the Head to Body.

Arms: Sew the Arms to either side of the Body, one round below the neckline.

Face:

- Using MC, thickly embroider the Nose between the 10th & 11th rounds up from neckline.

- Using Color A, embroider the Eyes between the 11th & 12th rounds up from neckline, with 12 stitches between them.

- Using Pink, embroider the Cheeks between the 10th & 11th rounds up from neckline, one stitch away from the outside of each Eye.

Hair Braids

- Position the Hair on the back of the Head, so that the front bangs are about 16 rounds above the neckline, and the back of the Hair touches the neckline. Sew in place.

- Cut 24 strands of Color A into 8" (20cm) lengths.
- Attach 12 strands on each side - with 17 stitches open across the front of the Hair.

- Braid the strands on each side, and using Color G, tie with a bow.

65

Skirt

1

- Cut a strip of fabric 17⅔" (45 cm) by 2" (5 cm).

2

- Sew the short sides together with a ¼" (0.7 cm) seam allowance.

3

- Fold and sew a ¼" (0.7 cm) hem around the bottom.

4

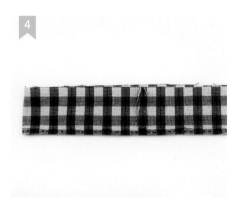

- Fold and sew a ¼" (0.7 cm) waist band around the top.

5

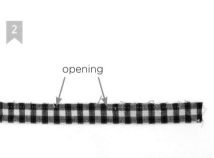

6

- Place Skirt on Body and fold pleats around, sewing to Round 34 (under Shirt detail).

Scarf

1

2

opening

3

- Trim the corners and turn inside out.

- Cut a strip of fabric 13⅔ (35 cm) by 2⅔" (7 cm). Fold in half lengthways and leaving and opening, sew as shown in photo.

4

- Trim the corners and turn inside out.

5

- Sew the opening closed to complete.

6

- Wrap around neck and tie in a knot.

Shoe Straps

- Sew a button to the outside of each shoe.

- Using Color G and yarn needle, make straps on both shoes. (photo 2 - 4)

- Using Color G and yarn needle, make straps on both shoes.

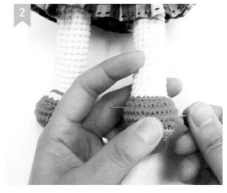

- Place the Hat on the Head.

ROBERT
the rabbit

ROBERT | Size (11" / 28 cm)

YARN: HELLO Cotton Yarn
- Main color (MC) - Gray (159)
- Color A - Off-White (155)
- Color B - Cherry Red (113)
- Color C - Navy Blue (153)
- Color D - Coral (111) 10g

HOOK: Size B-1 (2.25 mm) – or size suitable for yarn used.

OTHER: Yarn Needle
Embroidery Needle
Toy Stuffing
6 mm Round Black Button x 2 – for Eyes
13 mm Round Red Button x 1 – for Nose
10 mm Flat Brown Button x 2 – for Suspenders
Dark Brown Embroidery Thread
Beige Felt

PATTERN NOTE

All pieces are made in joined rounds, unless otherwise specified.

RABBIT

LEGS

First Leg

Round 1: Using MC, make an oval foundation chain of 6 stitches; starting in 2nd ch from hook, [sc in each of next 4 sts, inc in next st] 2 times. (12 sc)

Round 2: Inc in next st, sc in each of next 3 sts, inc in each of next 3 sts, sc in each of next 3 sts, inc in each of next 2 sts. (18 sc)

Round 3: Sc in next st, inc in next st, sc in each of next 3 sts, [sc in next st, inc in next st] 3 times, sc in each of next 3 sts, [sc in next st, inc in next st] 2 times. (24 sc)

Round 4: [Sc in each of next 3 sts, inc in next st] 6 times. (30 sc)

Rounds 5-7: *(3 rounds)* Sc in each st around. (30 sc)

Round 8: Sc in each of next 7 sts, [dec] 6 times, sc in each of next 11 sts. (24 sc)

Round 9: Sc in each st around. (24 sc)

Round 10: Sc in each of next 5 sts, [dec] 6 times, sc in each of next 7 sts. (18 sc)

Round 11: Sc in each st around. (18 sc)

Round 12: Sc in each of next 6 sts, [dec] 2 times, sc in each of next 8 sts. (16 sc)

Rounds 13-19: *(7 rounds)* Sc in each st around. (16 sc)

At the end of Round 19, fasten off.

Second Leg

Rounds 1-19: Repeat Rounds 1-19 of First Leg.

At the end of Round 19, continue with Body. (photo 1)

BODY

Round 20: *(Joining Legs)* Working on Second Leg, sc in each of next 12 sts *(4 sts remain unworked)*, ch 8; working on First Leg, sc in 5th st (photo 2), sc in each of next 15 sts; working in ch-8, sc in each of next 8 ch (photo 3); working on Second Leg, sc in next 4 sts. (40 sc)

Round 21: Sc in each of next 12 sts (photo 4); working in front loops only of ch-8, sc in each of next 8 ch; sc in each of next 28 sts. (48 sc) (photo 5)

Round 22: [Sc in each of next 7 sts, inc in next st] 6 times. (54 sc)

Round 23: Sc in each of next 4 sts, inc in next st, [sc in each of next 8 sts, inc in next st] 5 times, sc in each of next 4 sts. (60 sc)

Rounds 24-26: *(3 Rounds)* Sc in each st around. (60 sc)

For the following rounds, alternate Colors A & B every three rounds.

Rounds 27-29: *(3 Rounds)* Sc in each st around. (60 sc)

Round 30: Sc in each of next 9 sts, dec, [sc in each of next 18 sts, dec] 2 times, sc in each of next 9 sts. (57 sc)

Rounds 31-32: *(2 Rounds)* Sc in each st around. (57 sc)

Start stuffing, adding more as you go.

Round 33: [Sc in each of next 17 sts, dec] 3 times. (54 sc)

Round 34: Sc in each st around. (54 sc)

Round 35: Sc in each of next 8 sts, dec, [sc in each of next 16 sts, dec] 2 times, sc in each of next 8 sts. (51 sc)

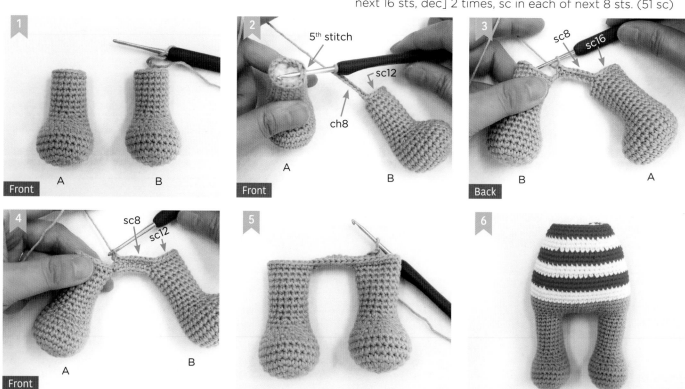

Round 36: Sc in each st around. (51 sc)

Round 37: [Sc in each of next 15 sts, dec] 3 times. (48 sc)

Round 38: Sc in each st around. (48 sc)

Round 39: Sc in each of next 7 sts, dec, [sc in each of next 14 sts, dec] 2 times, sc in each of next 7 sts. (45 sc)

Round 40: Sc in each st around. (45 sc)

Round 41: [Sc in each of next 13 sts, dec] 3 times. (42 sc)

Round 42: Sc in each st around. (42 sc)

Round 43: Sc in each of next 6 sts, dec, [sc in each of next 12 sts, dec] 2 times, sc in each of next 6 sts. (39 sc)

Round 44: [Sc in each of next 11 sts, dec] 3 times. (36 sc)

Continue stuffing. Fasten off. (photo 6)

HEAD

Round 1: Using MC, make an oval foundation chain of 12 stitches; starting in 2nd ch from hook, [sc in each of next 10 sts, inc in next st] 2 times. (24 sc)

Round 2: Inc in next st, sc in each of next 9 sts, inc in each of next 3 sts, sc in each of next 9 sts, inc in each of next 2 sts. (30 sc)

Round 3: Inc in next st, sc in each of next 12 sts, inc in each of next 3 sts, sc in each of next 12 sts, inc in each of next 2 sts. (36 sc)

Round 4: [Sc in each of next 15 sts, inc in each of next 3 sts] 2 times. (42 sc)

Round 5: Sc in each of next 17 sts, inc in each of next 3 sts, sc in each of next 18 sts, inc in each of next 3 sts, sc in next st. (48 sc)

Round 6: Sc in each of next 18 sts, inc in each of next 3 sts, sc in each of next 21 sts, inc in each of next 3 sts, sc in each of next 3 sts. (54 sc)

Round 7: Sc in each st around. (54 sc)

Round 8: Sc in each of next 21 sts, inc in each of next 3 sts, sc in each of next 24 sts, inc in each of next 3 sts, sc in each of next 3 sts. (60 sc)

Rounds 9-11: *(3 Rounds)* Sc in each st around. (60 sc)

Round 12: Sc in each of next 23 sts, inc in each of next 3 sts, sc in each of next 27 sts, inc in each of next 3 sts, sc in each of next 4 sts. (66 sc)

Rounds 13-16: *(4 Rounds)* Sc in each st around. (66 sc)

Round 17: Sc in each of next 25 sts, inc in each of next 3 sts, sc in each of next 30 sts, inc in each of next 3 sts, sc in each of next 5 sts. (72 sc)

Rounds 18-25: *(8 Rounds)* Sc in each st around. (72 sc)

Round 26: Sc in each of next 5 sts, dec, [sc in each of next 10 sts, dec] 5 times, sc in next 5 sts. (66 sc)

Round 27: [Sc in each of next 9 sts, dec] 6 times. (60 sc) Start stuffing, adding more as you go.

Round 28: Sc in each of next 4 sts, dec, [sc in each of next 8 sts, dec] 5 times, sc in next 4 sts. (54 sc)

Round 29: [Sc in each of next 7 sts, dec] 6 times. (48 sc)

Round 30: [Sc in each of next 2 sts, dec] 12 times. (36 sc) Fasten off, leaving a 20" (50 cm) long tail. (photo 7)

ARM (Make 2)

Round 1: Using MC, make a Magic Ring; 6 sc in ring. (6 sc)

Round 2: Inc in each st around. (12 sc)

Rounds 3-4: *(2 rounds)* Sc in each st around. (12 sc)

Round 5: Sc in each of next 5 sts, [(2 dc) in next st] 2 times, sc in each of next 5 sts. (10 sc & 4 dc)

Round 6: Sc in each of next 5 sts, [dec] 2 times, sc in each of next 5 sts. (12 sc)

For the following rounds, alternate Colors B & A every three rounds.

Rounds 7-20: *(14 Rounds)* Sc in each st around. (12 sc) Stuff the Arm about ⅔ full.

Round 21: [Sc in each of next 4 sts, dec] 2 times. (10 sc) Fasten off, leaving a 16" (40 cm) long tail. (photo 8)

EAR (Make 2)

Round 1: Using MC, make a Magic Ring; 6 sc in ring. (6 sc)

Round 2: Inc in each st around. (12 sc)

Round 3: [Sc in next st, inc in next st] 6 times. (18 sc)

Rounds 4-12: *(9 rounds)* Sc in each st around. (18 sc)

Round 13: [Sc in each of next 7 sts, dec] 2 times. (16 sc)

Round 14: Sc in each st around. (16 sc)

Round 15: [Sc in each of next 6 sts, dec] 2 times. (14 sc)

Round 16: Sc in each st around. (14 sc)

Fasten off, leaving a 20" (50 cm) long tail. (photo 9)

7

8

9

TAIL

Round 1: Using MC, make a Magic Ring; 6 sc in ring. (6 sc)

Round 2: Inc in each st around. (12 sc)

Rounds 3-4: *(2 rounds)* Sc in each st around. (12 sc)

Round 5: [Dec] 6 times. (6 sc)

Fasten off, leaving a 20" (50 cm) long tail. (photo 10)

CHEEK (Make 2)

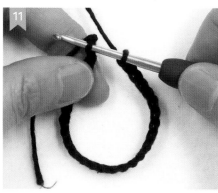

Round 1: Using Color D, make a Magic Ring; 6 sc in ring. (6 sc)

Round 2: Inc in each st around. (12 sc)

Round 3: [Sc in next st, inc in next st] 6 times. (18 sc)

Fasten off, leaving a 15¾" (50 cm) long tail.

OVERALLS

First Leg

Round 1: Using Color C, make a foundation chain of 30 stitches; join with sl st to first ch; ch 1, working in **back loops** only, sc in each ch around; join with sl st to first sc. (30 sc) (photos 11 & 12)

Rounds 2-6: *(5 rounds)* Sc in each st around. (30 sc)

At the end of Round 6, fasten off.

Second Leg

Rounds 1-6: Repeat Rounds 1-6 of First Leg.

At the end of Round 6, continue with Shorts. (photo 13)

Shorts

Round 7: *(Joining Legs)* Working on Second Leg, sc in each of next 25 sts *(5 sts remain unworked)*; working on First Leg, sc in 6th st (photo 14), sc in each of next 29 sts; working on Second Leg, sc in each of next 5 sts. (60 sc)

Rounds 8-12: *(5 Rounds)* Sc in each st around. (60 sc)

Round 13: Sc in each of next 53 sts, ch 4, skip next 4 sts *(tail hole made)*, sc in each of next 3 sts. (56 sc & ch-4)

Round 14: Sc in each st and ch around. (60 sc)

Rounds 15-16: *(2 Rounds)* Sc in each st around. (60 sc)

At the end of Round 16, fasten off and weave in ends. (photo 15)

Bib

With Shorts folded flat *(tail hole at center back)*, working across the stitches on the front, join Color C in 7th st from edge. (photo 16)

Row 1: Ch 1, sc in each of next 17 sts. (17 sc) Leave remaining sts unworked.

Rows 2-7: *(6 Rows)* Ch 1, turn, sc in each st across. (17 sc)

At the end of Row 7, fasten off and weave in ends.

Overall Strap (Make 2)

Row 1: Using Color C, ch 30, sc in 6th ch from hook *(skipped ch-5 is buttonhole)*, [sc in next ch] across. (25 sc)

Fasten off, leaving a 6" (15 cm) long tail.

Body: Position the Head on the Body with flat side as Face, and using the long tails, sew together.

Arms: Sew the Arms to either side of the Body, one round below the neckline.

Tail: Position Tail at center back of Body on Round 26, and sew in place.

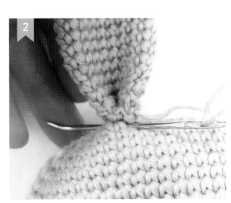

Ears: Fold the base of each Ear together and position at top of the Head on Round 1 – with 7 stitches between them. Using long tails, sew in place.

Face:

- Sew the Eye Buttons between Rounds 14 & 15 of Head, with 10 stitches between them.

- Sew the Nose button between the Eyes on Round 15 of Head.

- Using long tails, sew the Cheeks between Rounds 15 & 22 of Head, about 3 stitches out from each Eye.

- Using the Brown thread embroider the Mouth, and embroider the Eyebrows about five rounds above each Eye.

- Sew each Suspender Strap on either side at the back with 16 stitches between them. Cross the straps at the back and bring to the front.

- On the front, sew the Buttons to the Bib and fasten the suspenders to the buttons.

- Using Brown thread, sew the Felt Pocket to the Bib.

- Place Overalls on Rabbit.

Accessories:

HARRY
the happy puppy

HARRY | Size (9½" / 24 cm)

YARN: HELLO Cotton Yarn

- Main color (MC) - Dark Beige (158)
- Color A - Brown (126)
- Color B - Kelly Green (132)
- Color C - Navy Blue (153)
- Color D - Coral (111)

HOOK: Size B-1 (2.25 mm) – or size suitable for yarn used.

OTHER: Yarn Needle
Embroidery Needle
Toy Stuffing
6 mm Round Black Button x 2 – for Eyes
13 mm Round Dark Brown Button x 1 – for Nose
10 mm Flat Brown Button x 2 – for Suspenders
Dark Brown Embroidery Thread
Beige Felt

PATTERN NOTE

All pieces are made in joined rounds, unless otherwise specified.

PUPPY

LEGS

First Leg

Round 1: Using MC, make an oval foundation chain of 6 stitches; starting in 2nd ch from hook, [sc in each of next 4 sts, inc in next st] 2 times. (12 sc)

Round 2: Inc in next st, sc in each of next 3 sts, inc in each of next 3 sts, sc in each of next 3 sts, inc in each of next 2 sts. (18 sc)

Round 3: Sc in next st, inc in next st, sc in each of next 3 sts, [sc in next st, inc in next st] 3 times, sc in each of next 3 sts, [sc in next st, inc in next st] 2 times. (24 sc)

Round 4: [Sc in each of next 3 sts, inc in next st] 6 times. (30 sc)

Rounds 5-7: *(3 rounds)* Sc in each st around. (30 sc)

Round 8: Sc in each of next 7 sts, [dec] 6 times, sc in each of next 11 sts. (24 sc)

Round 9: Sc in each st around. (24 sc)

Round 10: Sc in each of next 5 sts, [dec] 6 times, sc in each of next 7 sts. (18 sc)

Round 11: Sc in each st around. (18 sc)

Round 12: Sc in each of next 6 sts, [dec] 2 times, sc in each of next 8 sts. (16 sc)

Rounds 13-19: *(7 rounds)* Sc in each st around. (16 sc)

At the end of Round 19, fasten off.

Second Leg

Rounds 1-19: Repeat Rounds 1-19 of First Leg.

At the end of Round 19, continue with Body. (photo 1)

BODY

Round 20: *(Joining Legs)* Working on Second Leg, sc in each of next 12 sts *(4 sts remain unworked)*, ch 8; working on First Leg, sc in 5th st (photo 2), sc in each of next 15 sts; working in ch-8, sc in each of next 8 ch (photo 3); working on Second Leg, sc in next 4 sts. (40 sc)

Round 21: Sc in each of next 12 sts (photo 4); working in front loops only of ch-8, sc in each of next 8 ch; sc in each of next 28 sts. (48 sc) (photo 5)

Round 22: [Sc in each of next 7 sts, inc in next st] 6 times. (54 sc)

Round 23: Sc in each of next 4 sts, inc in next st, [sc in each of next 8 sts, inc in next st] 5 times, sc in each of next 4 sts. (60 sc)

Rounds 24-26: *(3 Rounds)* Sc in each st around. (60 sc)

For the following rounds, alternate Colors A & B every three rounds.

Rounds 27-29: *(3 Rounds)* Sc in each st around. (60 sc)

Round 30: Sc in each of next 9 sts, dec, [sc in each of next 18 sts, dec] 2 times, sc in each of next 9 sts. (57 sc)

Rounds 31-32: *(2 Rounds)* Sc in each st around. (57 sc)

Start stuffing, adding more as you go.

Round 33: [Sc in each of next 17 sts, dec] 3 times. (54 sc)

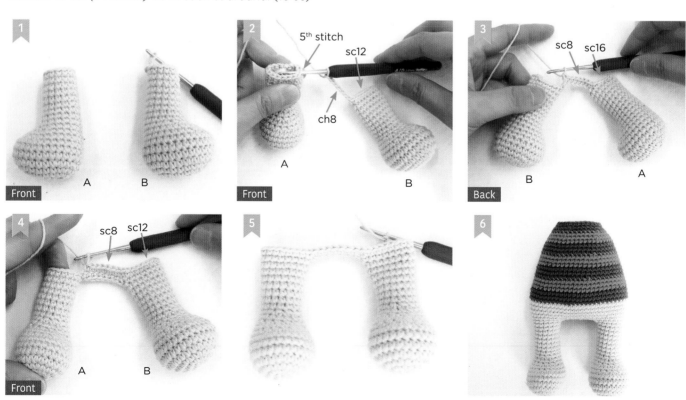

Round 34: Sc in each st around. (54 sc)

Round 35: Sc in each of next 8 sts, dec, [sc in each of next 16 sts, dec] 2 times, sc in each of next 8 sts. (51 sc)

Round 36: Sc in each st around. (51 sc)

Round 37: [Sc in each of next 15 sts, dec] 3 times. (48 sc)

Round 38: Sc in each st around. (48 sc)

Round 39: Sc in each of next 7 sts, dec, [sc in each of next 14 sts, dec] 2 times, sc in each of next 7 sts. (45 sc)

Round 40: Sc in each st around. (45 sc)

Round 41: [Sc in each of next 13 sts, dec] 3 times. (42 sc)

Round 42: Sc in each st around. (42 sc)

Round 43: Sc in each of next 6 sts, dec, [sc in each of next 12 sts, dec] 2 times, sc in each of next 6 sts. (39 sc)

Round 44: [Sc in each of next 11 sts, dec] 3 times. (36 sc)

Continue stuffing. Fasten off. *(photo 6)*

HEAD

Round 1: Using MC, make an oval foundation chain of 12 stitches; starting in 2nd ch from hook, [sc in each of next 10 sts, inc in next st] 2 times. (24 sc)

Round 2: Inc in next st, sc in each of next 9 sts, inc in each of next 3 sts, sc in each of next 9 sts, inc in each of next 2 sts. (30 sc)

Round 3: Inc in next st, sc in each of next 12 sts, inc in each of next 3 sts, sc in each of next 12 sts, inc in each of next 2 sts. (36 sc)

Round 4: [Sc in each of next 15 sts, inc in each of next 3 sts] 2 times. (42 sc)

Round 5: Sc in each of next 17 sts, inc in each of next 3 sts, sc in each of next 18 sts, inc in each of next 3 sts, sc in next st. (48 sc)

Round 6: Sc in each of next 18 sts, inc in each of next 3 sts, sc in each of next 21 sts, inc in each of next 3 sts, sc in each of next 3 sts. (54 sc)

Round 7: Sc in each st around. (54 sc)

Round 8: Sc in each of next 21 sts, inc in each of next 3 sts, sc in each of next 24 sts, inc in each of next 3 sts, sc in each of next 3 sts. (60 sc)

Rounds 9-11: *(3 Rounds)* Sc in each st around. (60 sc)

Round 12: Sc in each of next 23 sts, inc in each of next 3 sts, sc in each of next 27 sts, inc in each of next 3 sts, sc in each of next 4 sts. (66 sc)

Rounds 13-16: *(4 Rounds)* Sc in each st around. (66 sc)

Round 17: Sc in each of next 25 sts, inc in each of next 3 sts, sc in each of next 30 sts, inc in each of next 3 sts, sc in each of next 5 sts. (72 sc)

Rounds 18-25: *(8 Rounds)* Sc in each st around. (72 sc)

Round 26: Sc in each of next 5 sts, dec, [sc in each of next 10 sts, dec] 5 times, sc in next 5 sts. (66 sc)

Round 27: [Sc in each of next 9 sts, dec] 6 times. (60 sc)

Start stuffing, adding more as you go.

Round 28: Sc in each of next 4 sts, dec, [sc in each of next 8 sts, dec] 5 times, sc in next 4 sts. (54 sc)

Round 29: [Sc in each of next 7 sts, dec] 6 times. (48 sc)

Round 30: [Sc in each of next 2 sts, dec] 12 times. (36 sc)

Fasten off, leaving a 20" (50 cm) long tail. *(photos 7 & 8)*

ARM (Make 2)

Round 1: Using MC, make a Magic Ring; 6 sc in ring. (6 sc)

Round 2: Inc in each st around. (12 sc)

Rounds 3-4: *(2 rounds)* Sc in each st around. (12 sc)

Round 5: Sc in each of next 5 sts, [(2 dc) in next st] 2 times, sc in each of next 5 sts. (10 sc & 4 dc)

Round 6: Sc in each of next 5 sts, [dec] 2 times, sc in each of next 5 sts. (12 sc)

For the following rounds, alternate Colors B & A every three rounds.

Rounds 7-20: *(14 Rounds)* Sc in each st around. (12 sc)

Stuff the Arm about ⅔ full.

Round 21: [Sc in each of next 4 sts, dec] 2 times. (10 sc)

Fasten off, leaving a 16" (40 cm) long tail. *(photo 9)*

EAR (Make 2)

Round 1: Using Color A, make a Magic Ring; 6 sc in ring. (6 sc)

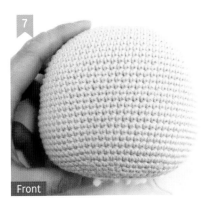

Front

Side

77

Round 2: Inc in each st around. (12 sc)

Round 3: [Sc in next st, inc in next st] 6 times. (18 sc)

Rounds 4-6: *(3 rounds)* Sc in each st around. (18 sc)

Round 7: [Sc in each of next 7 sts, dec] 2 times. (16 sc)

Round 8: Sc in each st around. (16 sc)

Round 9: [Sc in each of next 6 sts, dec] 2 times. (14 sc)

Round 10: Sc in each st around. (14 sc)

Round 11: [Sc in each of next 5 sts, dec] 2 times. (12 sc)

Round 12: Sc in each st around. (12 sc)

Fasten off, leaving a 20" (50 cm) long tail. (photo 10)

TAIL

Round 1: Using Color A, make a Magic Ring; 6 sc in ring. (6 sc)

Round 2: Inc in each st around. (12 sc)

Rounds 3-4: *(2 rounds)* Sc in each st around. (12 sc)

Round 5: [Sc in each of next 4 sts, dec] 2 times. (10 sc)

Round 6: Sc in each st around. (10 sc)

Round 7: [Sc in each of next 3 sts, dec] 2 times. (8 sc)

Round 8: Sc in each st around. (8 sc)

Fasten off, leaving a 16" (40 cm) long tail. (photo 11)

CHEEK (Make 2)

Round 1: Using Color D, make a Magic Ring; 6 sc in ring. (6 sc)

Round 2: Inc in each st around. (12 sc)

Fasten off, leaving a 16" (40 cm) long tail.

OVERALLS

First Leg

Round 1: Using Color C, make a foundation chain of 30 stitches; join with sl st to first ch; ch 1, working in **back loops** only, sc in each ch around; join with sl st to first sc. (30 sc) (photos 12 & 13)

Rounds 2-6: *(5 rounds)* Sc in each st around. (30 sc)

At the end of Round 6, fasten off.

Second Leg

Rounds 1-6: Repeat Rounds 1-6 of First Leg.

At the end of Round 6, continue with Shorts. (photo 14)

Shorts

Round 7: *(Joining Legs)* Working on Second Leg, sc in each of next 25 sts *(5 sts remain unworked)*; working on First Leg, sc in 6th st, sc in each of next 29 sts; working on Second Leg, sc in each of next 5 sts. (60 sc) (photo 15)

Rounds 8-12: *(5 Rounds)* Sc in each st around. (60 sc)

Round 13: Sc in each of next 53 sts, ch 4, skip next 4 sts *(tail hole made)*, sc in each of next 3 sts. (56 sc & ch-4)

Round 14: Sc in each st and ch around. (60 sc)

Rounds 15-16: *(2 Rounds)* Sc in each st around. (60 sc) (photo 16)

At the end of Round 16, fasten off and weave in ends.

Bib

With Shorts folded flat *(tail hole at center back)*, working across the stitches on the front, join Color C in 7th st from edge. (photo 17)

Row 1: Ch 1, sc in each of next 17 sts. (17 sc) Leave remaining sts unworked.

Rows 2-7: *(6 Rows)* Ch 1, turn, sc in each st across. (17 sc)

At the end of Row 7, fasten off and weave in ends.

Overall Strap (Make 2)

Row 1: Using Color C, ch 30, sc in 6th ch from hook *(skipped ch-5 is buttonhole)*, [sc in next ch] across. (25 sc)

Fasten off, leaving a 4" (10 cm) long tail.

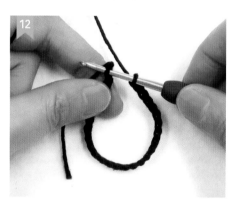

ASSEMBLY (use photos as guide)

Body: Position the Head on the Body with flat side as Face, and using the long tails, sew together.

Arms: Sew the Arms to either side of the Body, one round below the neckline.

Ears: Flatten each Ear and position on either side at top of the Head between Rounds 3 & 4. Using long tails, sew in place.

Tail: Position Tail at center back of Body between Rounds 26 & 27, and sew in place.

Face:

- Sew the Eye Buttons between Rounds 14 & 15 of Head, with 9 stitches between them.

- Sew the Nose button between the Eyes on Round 15 of Head.

- Using long tails, sew the Cheeks between Rounds 14 & 20 of Head, about 3 stitches out from each Eye.

- Using the Brown thread embroider the Mouth, and embroider the Eyebrows about three rounds above each Eye.

Accessories

- Sew each Suspender Strap on either side at the back with 16 stitches between them. Cross the straps at the back and bring to the front.

- On the front, sew the Buttons to the Bib and fasten the suspenders to the buttons.

- Using Brown thread, sew the Felt Pocket to the Bib.

- Place Overalls on Puppy.

ROCKY ROOSTER AND
the chicklets

ROCKY ROOSTER | Size (11″ / 28 cm)

YARN: HELLO Cotton Yarn
- Main color (MC) - Off-White (155)
- Color A - Yellow (123)
- Color B - Sky Blue (147)
- Color C - Baby Blue (146)
- Color D - Red (114)
- Color E - Kelly Green (132)

HOOK: Size B-1 (2.25 mm) – or size suitable for yarn used.

OTHER: Yarn Needle
Embroidery Needle
Toy Stuffing
Brown & Pink Embroidery Thread
Water Soluble Marker
10 mm Flat Wooden Button x 2

THE CHICKLETS | Size (3″ / 8 cm)

YARN: HELLO Cotton Yarn
- Main color (MC) - Off-White (155)
- Color A - Yellow (123)

HOOK: Size B-1 (2.25 mm) – or size suitable for yarn used.

OTHER: Yarn Needle
Embroidery Needle
Toy Stuffing
Brown & Pink Embroidery Thread

All pieces are made in joined rounds, unless otherwise specified.

SPECIAL STITCHES

Shell: Work 5 double crochet stitches in the same stitch or space specified.

ROOSTER

FIRST LEG

Toe (Make 3)

Round 1: Using Color A, make a Magic Ring; 6 sc in ring. (6 sc)

Rounds 2-6: *(5 rounds)* Sc in each st around. (6 sc)

At the end of Round 6, for the first two Toes, fasten off. For the third Toe, continue with Round 7. (photo 1)

Round 7: *(Joining Toes)* Working on Third Toe, sc in each of next 5 sts *(1 st remains unworked)*; working on Second Toe, sc in 2nd st (photo 2), sc in each of next 2 sts *(3 sts remain unworked)*; working in First Toe, sc in 2nd st (photo 3), sc in each of next 5 sts; working on Second Toe, sc in each of next 3 sts (photo 4); working on Third Toe, sc in next st. (18 sc) (photo 5)

Round 8: Sc in each st around. (18 sc)

Round 9: [Sc in each of next 4 sts, dec] 3 times. (15 sc)

Round 10: [Sc in each of next 3 sts, dec] 3 times. (12 sc)

Round 11: [Sc in each of next 2 sts, dec] 3 times. (9 sc)

Rounds 12-17: *(6 rounds)* Sc in each st around. (9 sc) (photo 6)

At the end of Round 17, change to MC.

Round 18: Inc in each st around. (18 sc)

Round 19: Sc in next st, inc in next st, [sc in each of next 2 sts, inc in next st] 5 times, sc in next st. (24 sc)

Round 20: [Sc in each of next 3 sts, inc in next st] 6 times. (30 sc)

Rounds 21-28: *(8 rounds)* Sc in each st around. (30 sc)

At the end of Round 28, fasten off.

Second Leg

Rounds 1-28: Repeat Rounds 1-28 of First Leg.

At the end of Round 28, continue with Body. (photo 7)

BODY & HEAD

Round 29: *(Joining Legs)* Working on Second Leg, sc in each of next 24 sts *(6 sts remain unworked)*, ch 3 (photo 8); working on First Leg, sc in 10th st (photo 9), sc in each of next 29 sts; working in ch-3, sc in each of next 3 ch (photo 10); working on Second Leg, sc in each of next 6 sts. (63 sc)

Round 30: Sc in each of next 24 sts; working in front loops only of ch-3, sc in each of next 3 ch; sc in each of next 39 sts. (66 sc) (photo 11)

Round 31: Sc in each of next 5 sts, inc in next st, [sc in each of next 10 sts, inc in next st] 5 times, sc in each of next 5 sts. (72 sc)

Round 32: [Sc in each of next 11 sts, inc in next st] 6 times. (78 sc)

Rounds 33-36: *(4 rounds)* Sc in each st around. (78 sc)

For the following rounds, alternate Colors B & C every three rounds.

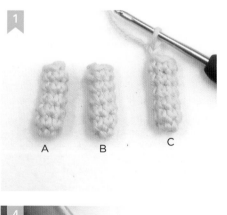

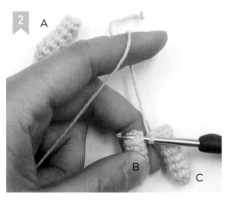

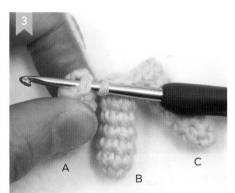

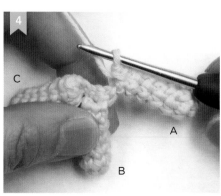

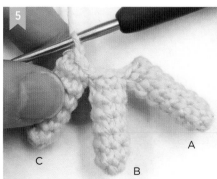

Rounds 37-39: *(3 rounds)* Sc in each st around. (78 sc)

Round 40: Sc in each of next 12 sts, dec, [sc in each of next 24 sts, dec] 2 times, sc in each of next 12 sts. (75 sc)

Rounds 41-42: *(2 rounds)* Sc in each st around. (75 sc)

Round 43: [Sc in each of next 23 sts, dec] 3 times. (72 sc)

Rounds 44-45: *(2 rounds)* Sc in each st around. (72 sc)

Round 46: Sc in each of next 11 sts, dec, [sc in each of next 22 sts, dec] 2 times, sc in each of next 11 sts. (69 sc)

Rounds 47-48: *(2 rounds)* Sc in each st around. (69 sc)

Round 49: [Sc in each of next 21 sts, dec] 3 times. (66 sc)

Rounds 50-51: *(2 rounds)* Sc in each st around. (66 sc)

Round 52: Sc in each of next 10 sts, dec, [sc in each of next 20 sts, dec] 2 times, sc in each of next 10 sts. (63 sc)

Rounds 53-54: *(2 rounds)* Sc in each st around. (63 sc)

At the end of Round 54, change to MC.

Round 55: [Sc in each of next 19 sts, dec] 3 times. (60 sc)

Round 56: Working in **back loops** only, sc in each st around. (60 sc)

Rounds 57-65: *(9 rounds)* Sc in each st around. (60 sc)

Round 66: Sc in each of next 14 sts, dec, sc in each of next 28 sts, dec, sc in each of next 14 sts. (58 sc)

Round 67: [Sc in each of next 27 sts, dec] 2 times. (56 sc)

Round 68: Sc in each of next 13 sts, dec, sc in each of next 26 sts, dec, sc in each of next 13 sts. (54 sc)

Round 69: [Sc in each of next 25 sts, dec] 2 times. (52 sc)

Round 70: Sc in each of next 12 sts, dec, sc in each of next 24 sts, dec, sc in each of next 12 sts. (50 sc)

Round 71: [Sc in each of next 23 sts, dec] 2 times. (48 sc)

Round 72: Sc in each of next 11 sts, dec, sc in each of next 22 sts, dec, sc in each of next 11 sts. (46 sc)

Round 73: [Sc in each of next 21 sts, dec] 2 times. (44 sc)

Round 74: Sc in each of next 10 sts, dec, sc in each of next 20 sts, dec, sc in each of next 10 sts. (42 sc)

Start stuffing, adding more as you go.

Round 75: [Sc in each of next 5 sts, dec] 6 times. (36 sc)

Round 76: Sc in each of next 2 sts, dec, [sc in each of next 4 sts, dec] 5 times, sc in each of next 2 sts. (30 sc)

Round 77: [Sc in each of next 3 sts, dec] 6 times. (24 sc)

Round 78: Sc in next st, dec, [sc in each of next 2 sts, dec] 5 times, sc in next st. (18 sc)

Round 79: [Sc in next st, dec] 6 times. (12 sc)

Finish stuffing.

Close the last round with a needle. Secure and weave in the end.

Neck Detail

Holding doll upside down, working in the front loops of Round 55, starting at the back, join MC to any st. (photo 12)

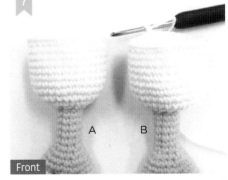

Round 1: Sc in each st around. (60 sc) (photos 13 & 14)

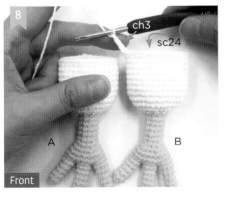

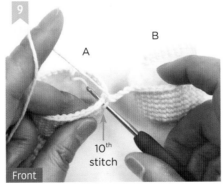

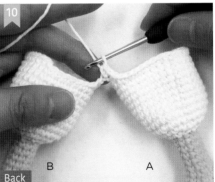

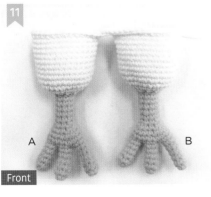

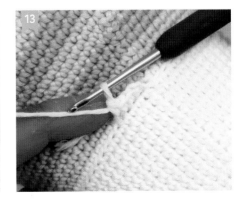

Round 2: [Sc in next st, skip next 2 sts, shell in next st, skip next 2 sts] 10 times. (10 shells) (photos 15 & 16)

Fasten off and weave in ends.

WING (Make 2)

Round 1: Using MC, make a Magic Ring; 6 sc in ring. (6 sc)

Round 2: Inc in next st, sc in each of next 4 sts, inc in next st. (8 sc)

Round 3: Inc in next st, sc in each of next 6 sts, inc in next st. (10 sc)

Round 4: Inc in next st, sc in each of next 8 sts, inc in next st. (12 sc)

Round 5: Inc in next st, sc in each of next 10 sts, inc in next st. (14 sc)

Round 6: Inc in next st, sc in each of next 12 sts, inc in next st. (16 sc)

Round 7: Inc in next st, sc in each of next 14 sts, inc in next st. (18 sc)

Round 8: Inc in next st, sc in each of next 16 sts, inc in next st. (20 sc)

Round 9: Inc in next st, sc in each of next 18 sts, inc in next st. (22 sc)

Rounds 10-12: (3 rounds) Sc in each st around. (22 sc)

Round 13: Dec, sc in each of next 18 sts, dec. (20 sc)

Round 14: Sc in each st around. (20 sc)

Round 15: Dec, sc in each of next 16 sts, dec. (18 sc)

Round 16: Sc in each st around. (18 sc)

Round 17: Dec, sc in each of next 14 sts, dec. (16 sc)

Round 18: Sc in each st around. (16 sc)

Round 19: Dec, sc in each of next 12 sts, dec. (14 sc)

Stuff the Wing about 2/3 full.

Fasten off, leaving a 16" (40 cm) long tail. (photo 17)

BEAK

Top/Bottom Beak (Make 2)

Round 1: Using Color A, make a Magic Ring; 6 sc in ring. (6 sc)

Round 2: Inc in each st around. (12 sc)

Rounds 3-6: (4 rounds) Sc in each st around. (12 sc)

Fasten off, leaving a 20" (50 cm) long tail.

Stuff each Beak piece.

COMB

First Piece

Round 1: Using Color D, make a Magic Ring; 6 sc in ring. (6 sc)

Round 2: Inc in each st around. (12 sc)

Rounds 3-6: (4 rounds) Sc in each st around. (12 sc)

At the end of Round 6, fasten off.

Second Piece

Rounds 1-5: Repeat Rounds 1-5 of First Piece.

At the end of Round 5, fasten off.

Third Piece

Rounds 1-4: Repeat Rounds 1-4 of First Piece.

At the end of Round 4, continue with Joining Round. (photo 18)

Joining Round: Working on Third Piece, sc in each of next 6 sts (6 sts remain unworked); working on Second Piece, sc in 2nd st (photo 19), sc in each of next 5 sts (6 sts remain); working on First Piece, sc in 2nd st (photo 20), sc in each of next 11 sts (photo 21); working on Second Piece, sc in each of remaining 6 sts, working on Third Piece, sc in each of remaining 6 sts. (36 sc)

Last Round: [Sc in each of next 4 sts, dec] 6 times. (30 sc) (photo 22)

Fasten off, leaving a 20" (50 cm) long tail.

Stuff the Comb.

TAIL FEATHERS

Feather (Make 3)

Round 1: Using Color E, make a Magic Ring; 6 sc in ring. (6 sc)

Round 2: Inc in each st around. (12 sc)

Rounds 3-4: (2 rounds) Sc in each st around. (12 sc)

Round 5: [Sc in each of next 2 sts, dec] 3 times. (9 sc)

Round 6: Sc in each st around. (9 sc)

Round 7: [Sc in next st, dec] 3 times. (6 sc)

At the end of Round 7, for the first two Feathers, fasten off. For the third Feather, continue with Round 8. (photo 23)

Round 8: (Joining Round) Working on third Feather, sc in each of next 3 sts (3 sts remain unworked); working on second Feather, sc in 2nd st, sc in each of next 2 sts (3 sts remain); working on first Feather, sc in 2nd st, sc in each of next 5 sts; working on second Feather, sc in each of remaining 3 sts; working on third Feather, sc in each of remaining 3 sts. (18 sc) (photos 24-28)

Round 9: [Sc in next st, dec] 6 times. (12 sc)

Fasten off, leaving a 16" (40 cm) long tail.

Stuff the Feathers.

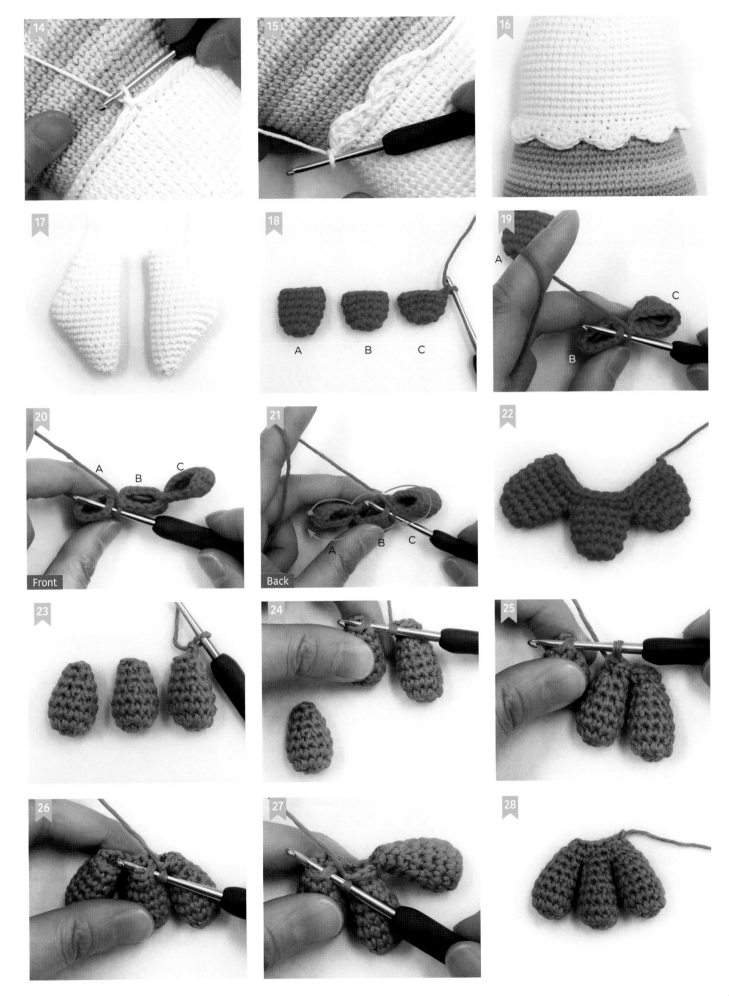

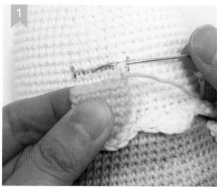

Wings: Flatten each Wing and with the straight side to the front, sew to either side of the Body between Rounds 51 & 52.

Beak: Mark the position of the Beak at the center of the Face between Rounds 61 & 62. Flatten each Beak piece and first sew the Bottom Beak to the marked position, then sew the Top Beak.

Comb: Mark the position of the Comb at the center top of Head - the line extends from Round 78 in the front, to Round 70 at the back. Flatten the Comb, and with the longer piece to the front, sew to the marked line.

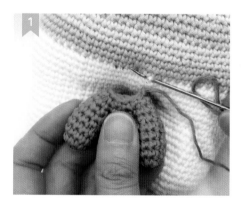

Tail Feathers: Mark the position of center back of Body between Rounds 36 & 37. Flatten and sew in place.

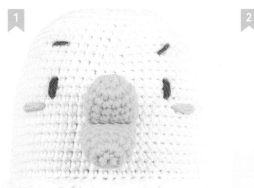 

Face:

- Using Brown embroidery thread, embroider the Eyes between Rounds 65 & 66 on the Body/Head, with 13 stitches between them.

- Embroider the Eyebrows above the Eyes on Round 70.

- Using Pink embroidery thread, embroider the Cheeks between Rounds 63 & 64, one stitch away from the outside of each Eye.

Accessories:

- Sew the Buttons to the front of Body.

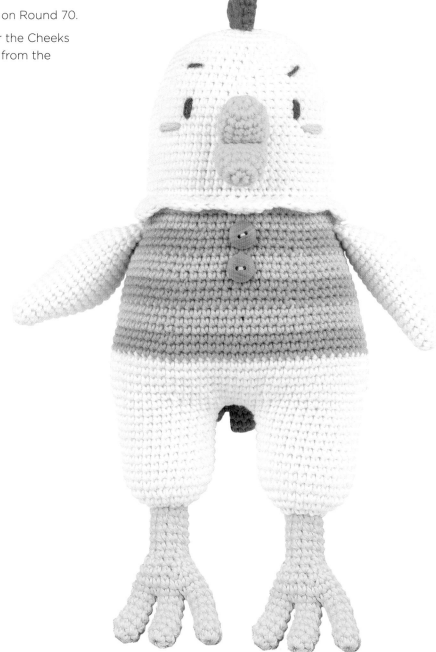

CHICK

HEAD & BODY

Round 1: Using Color A, make a Magic Ring; 6 sc in ring. (6 sc)

Round 2: Inc in each st around. (12 sc)

Round 3: [Sc in next st, inc in next st] 6 times. (18 sc)

Round 4: Sc in next st, inc in next st, [sc in each of next 2 sts, inc in next st] 5 times, sc in next st. (24 sc)

Round 5: [Sc in each of next 3 sts, inc in next st] 6 times. (30 sc)

Round 6: Sc in each of next 2 sts, inc in next st, [sc in each of next 4 sts, inc in next st] 5 times, sc in each of next 2 sts. (36 sc)

Round 7: Sc in each st around. (36 sc)

Round 8: [Sc in each of next 5 sts, inc in next st] 6 times. (42 sc)

Rounds 9-14: *(6 rounds)* Sc in each st around. (42 sc)

Round 15: Sc in each of next 3 sts, inc in next st, [sc in each of next 6 sts, inc in next st] 5 times, sc in each of next 3 sts. (48 sc)

Round 16: [Sc in each of next 7 sts, inc in next st] 6 times. (54 sc)

Rounds 17-22: *(6 rounds)* Sc in each st around. (54 sc)

Round 23: [Sc in each of next 7 sts, dec] 6 times. (48 sc)

Round 24: Sc in each of next 3 sts, dec, [sc in each of next 6 sts, dec] 5 times, sc in next 3 sts. (42 sc)

Round 25: [Sc in each of next 5 sts, dec] 6 times. (36 sc)

Round 26: Sc in each of next 2 sts, dec, [sc in each of next 4 sts, dec] 5 times, sc in next 2 sts. (30 sc)

Start stuffing, adding more as you go.

Round 27: [Sc in each of next 3 sts, dec] 6 times. (24 sc)

Round 28: Sc in next st, dec, [sc in each of next 2 sts, dec] 5 times, sc in next st. (18 sc)

Round 29: [Sc in next st, dec] 6 times. (12 sc)

Finish stuffing.

Close the last round with a needle. Secure and weave in the end. (photo 1)

WING (Make 2)

Round 1: Using Color A, make a Magic Ring; 6 sc in ring. (6 sc)

Round 2: Inc in next st, sc in each of next 4 sts, inc in next st. (8 sc)

Round 3: Inc in next st, sc in each of next 6 sts, inc in next st. (10 sc)

Rounds 4-6: *(3 rounds)* Sc in each st around. (10 sc)

Round 7: Dec, sc in each of next 6 sts, dec. (8 sc)

Stuff the Wing about ⅔ full.

Fasten off, leaving a 16" (40 cm) long tail. (photo 2)

BEAK

Round 1: Using MC, make a Magic Ring; 6 sc in ring. (6 sc)

Round 2: Inc in each st around. (12 sc)

Fasten off, leaving a 16" (40 cm) long tail.

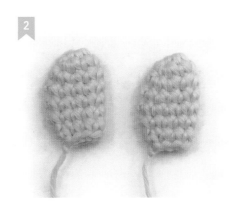

ASSEMBLY (use photos as guide)

Beak: Position of the Beak between Rounds 11 & 12, and sewing only across the diameter, sew in place.

Wings: Flatten each Wing and sew to either side of the Body between Rounds 13 & 14.

Hair: Using a short strand of Color A, fold in half and tie to top of Head.

Face:

- Using Brown embroidery thread, embroider the Eyes on Round 11, with 7 stitches between them.

- Using Pink embroidery thread, embroider the Cheeks between Rounds 12 & 13, one stitch away from the outside of each Eye.

KENNETH CARROT & BENJAMIN BROCCOLI
the smart vegetables

KENNETH CARROT | Size (6½" / 17 cm)

YARN: HELLO Cotton Yarn
- Color A - Dark Brown (127)
- Color B - Sage (137)
- Color C - Orange (119)
- Color D - Mocha (125)

HOOK: Size B-1 (2.25 mm) – or size suitable for yarn used.

OTHER: Yarn Needle
Embroidery Needle
Toy Stuffing
6 mm Round Black Button x 2 – for Eyes
Brown, Pink & Red Embroidery Thread

BENJAMIN BROCCOLI | Size (5½" / 14 cm)

YARN: HELLO Cotton Yarn
- Color A - Dark Brown (127)
- Color B - Sage (137)
- Color E - Dark Green (135)

HOOK: Size B-1 (2.25 mm) – or size suitable for yarn used.

OTHER: Yarn Needle
Embroidery Needle
Toy Stuffing
6 mm Round Black Button x 2 – for Eyes
Brown & Pink Embroidery Thread

PATTERN NOTE

All pieces are made in joined rounds, unless otherwise specified.

SPECIAL STITCHES

Back Post Single Crochet (BPsc): Insert the hook from back to front to back around the post of the specified stitch and pull up a loop *(2 loops on hook)*. Yarn over and draw through both loops on the hook.

Note: A post stitch is worked under the top loops of a stitch, around the post (vertical part) of the stitch.

CARROT

LEGS

First Leg

Round 1: Using Color A, make a Magic Ring; 6 sc in ring. (6 sc)

Round 2: Inc in each st around. (12 sc)

Rounds 3-5: *(3 rounds)* Sc in each st around. (12 sc)

Change to Color C.

Rounds 6-8: *(3 rounds)* Sc in each st around. (12 sc)

At the end of Round 8, fasten off.

Second Leg

Rounds 1-8: Repeat Rounds 1-8 of First Leg.

At the end of Round 8, continue with Body. (photo 1)

BODY & HEAD

Round 9: *(Joining Legs)* Working on Second Leg, sc in each of next 11 sts *(1 st remains unworked)*, ch 6; working on First Leg, sc in 2nd st (photo 2), sc in each of next 11 sts; working in ch-6, sc in each of next 6 ch (photo 3); working on Second Leg, sc in next st. (30 sc)

Round 10: Sc in each of next 11 sts; working in front loops only of ch-6, sc in each of next 6 ch (photo 4); sc in each of next 19 sts. (36 sc) (photo 5)

Round 11: [Sc in each of next 11 sts, inc in next st] 3 times. (39 sc)

Round 12: Sc in each st around. (39 sc)

Round 13: Sc in each of next 6 sts, inc in next st, [sc in each of next 12 sts, inc in next st] 2 times, sc in each of next 6 sts. (42 sc)

Round 14: Sc in each st around. (42 sc)

Round 15: [Sc in each of next 13 sts, inc in next st] 3 times. (45 sc)

Round 16: Sc in each st around. (45 sc)

Round 17: Sc in each of next 7 sts, inc in next st, [sc in each of next 14 sts, inc in next st] 2 times, sc in each of next 7 sts. (48 sc)

Round 18: [Sc in each of next 15 sts, inc in next st] 3 times. (51 sc)

Round 19: Sc in each of next 8 sts, inc in next st, [sc in each of next 16 sts, inc in next st] 2 times, sc in each of next 8 sts. (54 sc)

Round 20: [Sc in each of next 17 sts, inc in next st] 3 times. (57 sc)

Rounds 21-27: *(7 Rounds)* Sc in each st around. (57 sc)

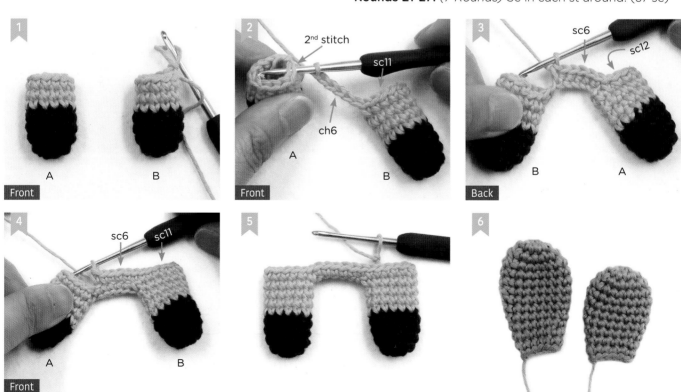

Round 28: [Sc in each of next 17 sts, dec] 3 times. (54 sc)

Round 29: [Sc in each of next 25 sts, dec] 2 times. (52 sc)

Round 30: Sc in each of next 12 sts, dec, sc in each of next 24 sts, dec, sc in each of next 12 sts. (50 sc)

Round 31: [Sc in each of next 23 sts, dec] 2 times. (48 sc)

Round 32: Sc in each of next 11 sts, dec, sc in each of next 22 sts, dec, sc in each of next 11 sts. (46 sc)

Round 33: [Sc in each of next 21 sts, dec] 2 times. (44 sc)

Round 34: Sc in each of next 10 sts, dec, sc in each of next 20 sts, dec, sc in each of next 10 sts. (42 sc)

Round 35: [Sc in each of next 5 sts, dec] 6 times. (36 sc)

Start stuffing, adding more as you go.

Round 36: Sc in each of next 2 sts, dec, [sc in each of next 4 sts, dec] 5 times, sc in each of next 2 sts. (30 sc)

Round 37: [Sc in each of next 3 sts, dec] 6 times. (24 sc)

Round 38: Sc in next st, dec, [sc in each of next 2 sts, dec] 5 times, sc in next st. (18 sc)

Round 39: [Sc in next st, dec] 6 times. (12 sc)

Finish stuffing.

Close the last round with a needle. Secure and weave in the end.

ARM (Make 2)

Round 1: Using Color C, make a Magic Ring; 6 sc in ring. (6 sc)

Round 2: [Sc in each of next 2 sts, inc in next st] 2 times. (8 sc)

Rounds 3-8: *(6 rounds)* Sc in each st around. (8 sc)

Stuff the Arm about ⅔ full.

Fasten off, leaving a 16" (40 cm) long tail.

CARROT TOP

Long Frond

Round 1: Using Color B, make a Magic Ring; 6 sc in ring. (6 sc)

Round 2: Inc in each st around. (12 sc)

Round 3: [Sc in next st, inc in next st] 6 times. (18 sc)

Rounds 4-7: *(4 rounds)* Sc in each st around. (18 sc)

Round 8: [Sc in each of next 7 sts, dec] 2 times. (16 sc)

Round 9: Sc in each st around. (16 sc)

Round 10: [Sc in each of next 6 sts, dec] 2 times. (14 sc)

Round 11: Sc in each st around. (14 sc)

Round 12: [Sc in each of next 5 sts, dec] 2 times. (12 sc)

Round 13: Sc in each st around. (12 sc)

Fasten off, leaving a 16" (40 cm) long tail. (photo 6)

Short Frond

Round 1: Using Color B, make a Magic Ring; 6 sc in ring. (6 sc)

Round 2: Inc in each st around. (12 sc)

Round 3: [Sc in next st, inc in next st] 6 times. (18 sc)

Rounds 4-5: *(2 rounds)* Sc in each st around. (18 sc)

Round 6: [Sc in each of next 7 sts, dec] 2 times. (16 sc)

Round 7: Sc in each st around. (16 sc)

Round 8: [Sc in each of next 6 sts, dec] 2 times. (14 sc)

Round 9: Sc in each st around. (14 sc)

Round 10: [Sc in each of next 5 sts, dec] 2 times. (12 sc)

Round 11: Sc in each st around. (12 sc)

Fasten off, leaving a 16" (40 cm) long tail. (photo 6)

VEST

Row 1: Using Color D, ch 31, sc in 2nd ch from hook, [sc in next ch] across. (30 sc)

Row 2: Ch 1, turn, sc in each st across (30 sc)

Row 3: Ch 1, turn, sc in each of next 4 sts, ch 8, skip next st, sc in each of next 20 sts, ch 8, skip next st, sc in each of next 4 sts. (28 sc & 2 ch-8)

Row 4: Ch 1, turn, sc in each of next 4 sts, sc in each of next 8 ch (photo 7), sc in each of next 20 sts, sc in each of next 8 ch, sc in each of next 4 sts. (44 sc)

Fasten off and weave in all ends. (photo 8)

BASKET

Round 1: Using Color D, make a Magic Ring; 7 sc in ring. (7 sc)

Round 2: Inc in each st around. (14 sc)

Round 3: [Sc in next st, inc in next st] 7 times. (21 sc)

Round 4: Sc in next st, inc in next st, [sc in each of next 2 sts, inc in next st] 6 times, sc in next st. (28 sc)

Round 5: BPsc in each st around. (28 sc)

Round 6: Sc in each st around. (28 sc)

Round 7: Sc in each of next 3 sts, inc in next st, [sc in each of next 6 sts, inc in next st] 3 times, sc in each of next 3 sts. (32 sc)

Round 8: Sc in each st around. (32 sc)

Round 9: Sc in each of next 7 sts, ch 5, skip next 2 sts, sc in each of next 14 sts, ch 5, skip next 2 sts, sc in each of next 7 sts. (28 sc & 2 ch-5)

Fasten off and weave in all ends. (photos 9 & 10)

MINI CARROT (Make 2 or more)

Round 1: Using Color C, make a Magic Ring; 6 sc in ring. (6 sc)

Round 2: [Sc in next st, inc in next st] 3 times (9 sc)

Round 3: Sc in each st around. (9 sc)

Round 4: Sc in next st, inc in next st, [sc in each of next 2 sts, inc in next st] 2 times, sc in next st. (12 sc)

Round 5: Sc in each st around. (12 sc)

Round 6: [Sc in each of next 3 sts, inc in next st] 3 times. (15 sc)

Round 7: Sc in each of next 2 sts, inc in next st, [sc in each of next 4 sts, inc in next st] 2 times, sc in each of next 2 sts. (18 sc)

Rounds 8-9: *(2 rounds)* Sc in each st around. (18 sc)

Round 10: [Sc in next st, dec] 6 times. (12 sc)

Start stuffing, adding more as you go.

Round 11: [Dec] 6 times. (6 sc)

Change to Color B.

Round 12: [Sc in next st, ch 6] 6 times. (6 sc & 6 ch-6)

Close the last round with a needle. Secure and weave in the end. (photo 11)

ASSEMBLY (use photos as guide)

Arms: Sew the Arms to either side of the Body, between Rounds 16 & 18.

Face:

- Sew the Eye Buttons between Rounds 26 & 27 with 10 stitches between them.

- Using the Brown thread, embroider the Eyebrows above each Eye between Rounds 30 & 31.

- Embroider the Mouth over Rounds 23-25.

- Using the Red thread, embroider the Nose between Rounds 25 & 26.

- Using Pink thread, embroider the Cheeks between Rounds 24 & 25, one stitch away from the outside of each Eye.

Carrot Top: Sew the Fronds to the top of the Head.

Accessories

- Place Vest on Carrot.

- Place the Mini-Carrots in the Basket

BROCCOLI

LEGS

First Leg

Round 1: Using Color A, make a Magic Ring; 6 sc in ring. (6 sc)

Round 2: Inc in each st around. (12 sc)

Rounds 3-5: *(3 rounds)* Sc in each st around. (12 sc)
Change to Color B.

Rounds 6-8: *(3 rounds)* Sc in each st around. (12 sc)
At the end of Round 8, fasten off.

Second Leg

Rounds 1-8: Repeat Rounds 1-8 of First Leg.
At the end of Round 8, continue with Body. (photo 1)

BODY

Round 9: *(Joining Legs)* Working on Second Leg, sc in each of next 11 sts *(1 st remains unworked)*, ch 6; working on First Leg, sc in 2nd st (photo 2), sc in each of next 11 sts; working in ch-6, sc in each of next 6 ch (photo 3); working on Second Leg, sc in next st. (30 sc)

Round 10: Sc in each of next 11 sts; working in front loops only of ch-6, sc in each of next 6 ch (photo 4); sc in each of next 19 sts. (36 sc) (photo 5)

Round 11: [Sc in each of next 11 sts, inc in next st] 3 times. (39 sc)

Round 12: Sc in each st around. (39 sc)

Round 13: Sc in each of next 6 sts, inc in next st, [sc in each of next 12 sts, inc in next st] 2 times, sc in each of next 6 sts. (42 sc)

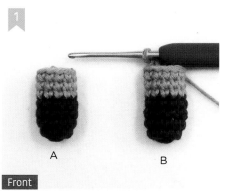

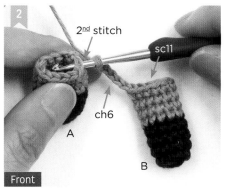

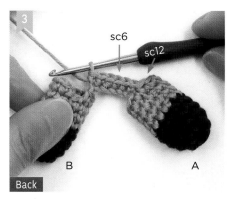

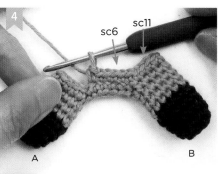

Round 14: Sc in each st around. (42 sc)

Round 15: [Sc in each of next 13 sts, inc in next st] 3 times. (45 sc)

Round 16: Sc in each st around. (45 sc)

Round 17: Sc in each of next 7 sts, inc in next st, [sc in each of next 14 sts, inc in next st] 2 times, sc in each of next 7 sts. (48 sc)

Round 18: [Sc in each of next 15 sts, inc in next st] 3 times. (51 sc)

Round 19: Sc in each of next 8 sts, inc in next st, [sc in each of next 16 sts, inc in next st] 2 times, sc in each of next 8 sts. (54 sc)

Round 20: [Sc in each of next 17 sts, inc in next st] 3 times. (57 sc)

Rounds 21-27: *(7 Rounds)* Sc in each st around. (57 sc)

Round 28: [Sc in each of next 17 sts, dec] 3 times. (54 sc)

Round 29: [Sc in each of next 25 sts, dec] 2 times. (52 sc)

Round 30: Sc in each of next 12 sts, dec, sc in each of next 24 sts, dec, sc in each of next 12 sts. (50 sc)

Round 31: Working in **back loops** only, [sc in each of next 23 sts, dec] 2 times. (48 sc)

Round 32: Sc in each of next 11 sts, dec, sc in each of next 22 sts, dec, sc in each of next 11 sts. (46 sc)

Round 33: Working in **back loops** only, [sc in each of next 21 sts, dec] 2 times. (44 sc)

Round 34: Sc in each of next 10 sts, dec, sc in each of next 20 sts, dec, sc in each of next 10 sts. (42 sc)

Round 35: Working in **back loops** only, [sc in each of next 5 sts, dec] 6 times. (36 sc)

Start stuffing, adding more as you go.

Round 36: Sc in each of next 2 sts, dec, [sc in each of next 4 sts, dec] 5 times, sc in each of next 2 sts. (30 sc)

Round 37: Working in **back loops** only, [sc in each of next 3 sts, dec] 6 times. (24 sc)

Round 38: Sc in next st, dec, [sc in each of next 2 sts, dec] 5 times, sc in next st. (18 sc)

Round 39: Working in **back loops** only, [sc in next st, dec] 6 times. (12 sc)

Finish stuffing.

Close the last round with a needle. Secure and weave in the end.

HAIR

Holding Toy upside down, working in the front loops of Rounds 30, 32, 34, 36, & 38, in a continuous spiral; join Color E to first st on Round 30; ch 1, sc in same st as joining; ch 10, [sc in next st, ch 10] around to the last stitch on Round 38.

Fasten off and weave in all ends. (photos 6-11)

ARM (Make 2)

Round 1: Using Color B, make a Magic Ring; 6 sc in ring. (6 sc)

Round 2: [Sc in each of next 2 sts, inc in next st] 2 times. (8 sc)

Rounds 3-8: *(6 rounds)* Sc in each st around. (8 sc)

Stuff the Arm about ⅔ full.

Fasten off, leaving a 16" (40 cm) long tail. (photo 12)

VEST

Row 1: Using Color A, ch 31, sc in 2nd ch from hook, [sc in next ch] across. (30 sc)

Row 2: Ch 1, turn, sc in each st across (30 sc)

Row 3: Ch 1, turn, sc in each of next 4 sts, ch 8, skip next st, sc in each of next 20 sts, ch 8, skip next st, sc in each of next 4 sts. (28 sc & 2 ch-8)

Row 4: Ch 1, turn, sc in each of next 4 sts, sc in each of next 8 ch, sc in each of next 20 sts, sc in each of next 8 ch, sc in each of next 4 sts. (44 sc)

Fasten off and weave in all ends. (photo 13)

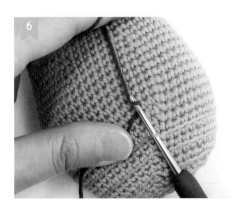
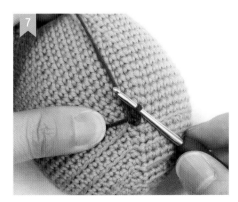

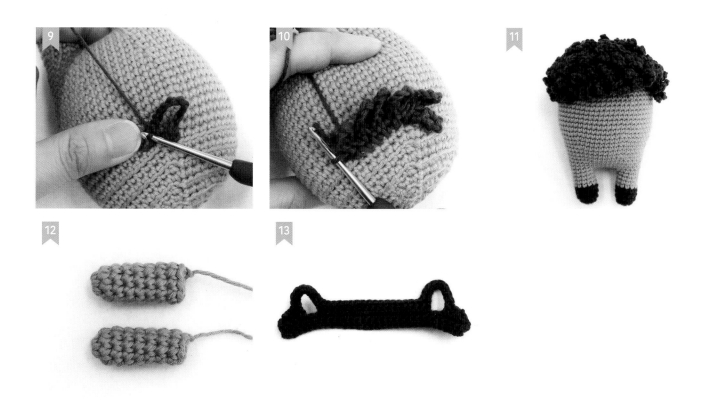

Arms: Sew the Arms to either side of the Body, between Rounds 16 & 18

Face:

- Sew the Eye Buttons between Rounds 23 & 24 with 11 stitches between them.

- Using the Brown thread, embroider the Eyebrows above each Eye between Rounds 26 & 27.

- Embroider the Mouth over Rounds 21-23.

- Using the Color E, embroider the Nose between Rounds 23 & 24.

- Using Pink thread, embroider the Cheeks between Rounds 21 & 22, one stitch away from the outside of each Eye.

ASSEMBLY (use photos as guide)

Accessories:

- Place Vest on Broccoli.

ZACK & ZOË
the cute couple

ZACK | Size (6½" / 17 cm)	**ZOË** | Size (6⅓" / 16 cm)
YARN: HELLO Cotton Yarn	**YARN:** HELLO Cotton Yarn
⬭ Main color (MC) - Powder Pink (162)	⬭ Main color (MC) - Powder Pink (162)
▬ Color A - Mustard (124)	▬ Color A - Mustard (124)
▬ Color B - Red (114)	▬ Color B - Red (114)
▬ Color C - Baby Blue (146)	▬ Color C - Baby Blue (146)
⬭ Color D - Off-White (155)	⬭ Color D - Off-White (155)
▬ Color E - Gray (159)	▬ Color E - Gray (159)
HOOK: Size B-1 (2.25 mm) or size suitable for yarn used.	**HOOK:** Size B-1 (2.25 mm) – or size suitable for yarn used.
OTHER: Yarn Needle Embroidery Needle Toy Stuffing 6 mm Flat White Button x 2 – for Suspenders Dark Brown and Pink Thread for Embroidery Grey Felt – for Pocket	**OTHER:** Yarn Needle Embroidery Needle Toy Stuffing 6 mm Flat White Button x 2 – for Suspenders Dark Brown and Pink Thread for Embroidery

PATTERN NOTE

All pieces are made in joined rounds, unless otherwise specified.

BOY

LEGS

First Leg

Round 1: Using Color E, make a Magic Ring; 6 sc in ring. (6 sc)

Round 2: Inc in each st around. (12 sc)

Rounds 3-4: *(2 rounds)* Sc in each st around. (12 sc)

Change to Color B.

Rounds 5-7: *(3 rounds)* Sc in each st around. (12 sc)

At the end of Round 7, fasten off.

Second Leg

Rounds 1-7: Repeat Rounds 1-7 of First Leg.

At the end of Round 7, continue with Body. (photo 1)

BODY

Round 8: *(Joining Legs)* Working on Second Leg, sc in each of next 11 sts *(1 st remains unworked)*, ch 6; working on First Leg, sc in 2nd st (photo 2), sc in each of next 11 sts; working in ch-6, sc in each of next 6 ch (photo 3); working on Second Leg, sc in next st. (30 sc)

Round 9: Sc in each of next 11 sts; working in front loops only of ch-6, sc in each of next 6 ch (photo 4); sc in each of next 19 sts. (36 sc) (photo 5)

Round 10: [Sc in each of next 5 sts, inc in next st] 6 times. (42 sc)

Rounds 11-15: *(5 Rounds)* Sc in each st around. (42 sc)

For the following rounds, alternate Colors C & D every round.

Round 16: Sc in each of next 12 sts, working in **back loops** only, sc in each of next 11 sts, *(working in both loops)* sc in each of next 19 sts. (42 sc)

Round 17: [Sc in each of next 19 sts, dec] 2 times. (40 sc)

Round 18: Sc in each st around. (40 sc)

Round 19: Sc in each of next 9 sts, dec, sc in each of next 18 sts, dec, sc in each of next 9 sts. (38 sc)

Round 20: [Sc in each of next 17 sts, dec] 2 times. (36 sc)

Start stuffing, adding more as you go.

Round 21: Sc in each of next 8 sts, dec, sc in each of next 16 sts, dec, sc in each of next 8 sts. (34 sc)

Round 22: [Sc in each of next 15 sts, dec] 2 times. (32 sc)

Round 23: Sc in each of next 7 sts, dec, sc in each of next 14 sts, dec, sc in each of next 7 sts. (30 sc)

Round 24: [Sc in each of next 13 sts, dec] 2 times. (28 sc)

Round 25: Sc in each of next 6 sts, dec, sc in each of next 12 sts, dec, sc in each of next 6 sts. (26 sc)

Round 26: [Sc in each of next 11 sts, dec] 2 times. (24 sc)

Continue stuffing. Fasten off. (photo 6)

Bib

Row 1: Working in front loops on Round 15 of Body, join

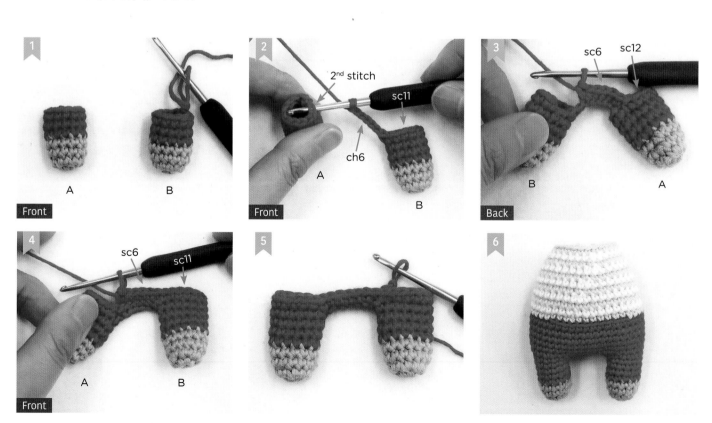

Color B to first st (photo 7), ch 1, sc in same st as joining, sc in each of next 10 sts. (11 sc) (photo 8)

Rows 2-5: *(4 rows)* Ch 1, turn, sc in each st across. (11 sc)

At the end of Row 5, fasten off, weaving in the ends. (photo 9)

ARM (Make 2)

Round 1: Using MC, make a Magic Ring; 6 sc in ring. (6 sc)

Round 2: [Sc in next st, inc in next st] 3 times. (9 sc)

Rounds 3-4: *(2 rounds)* Sc in each st around. (9 sc)

For the following rounds, alternate Colors C & D every round.

Rounds 5-11: *(7 rounds)* Sc in each st around. (9 sc)

Stuff the Arm about 2/3 full.

Round 12: [Sc in next st, dec] 3 times. (6 sc)

Fasten off, leaving a 16" (40 cm) long tail. (photo 10)

HEAD

Round 1: Using MC, make an oval foundation chain of 6 stitches; starting in 2nd ch from hook, [sc in each of next 4 sts, inc in next st] 2 times. (12 sc)

Round 2: Inc in next st, sc in each of next 3 sts, inc in each of next 3 sts, sc in each of next 3 sts, inc in each of next 2 sts. (18 sc)

Round 3: Sc in next st, inc in next st, sc in each of next 3 sts, [sc in next st, inc in next st] 3 times, sc in each of next 3 sts, [sc in next st, inc in next st] 2 times. (24 sc)

Round 4: Sc in next st, inc in next st, sc in each of next 4 sts, [sc in next st, inc in next st, sc in next st] 3 times, sc in each of next 3 sts, [sc in next st, inc in next st, sc in next st] 2 times. (30 sc)

Round 5: Sc in each of next 3 sts, inc in next st, sc in each of next 3 sts, [sc in each of next 3 sts, inc in next st] 3 times, sc in each of next 3 sts, [sc in each of next 3 sts, inc in next st] 2 times. (36 sc)

Round 6: [Sc in each of next 5 sts, inc in next st] 6 times. (42 sc)

Round 7: Sc in each of next 3 sts, inc in next st, [sc in each of next 6 sts, inc in next st] 5 times, sc in each of next 3 sts. (48 sc)

Round 8: [Sc in each of next 7 sts, inc in next st] 6 times. (54 sc)

Round 9: Sc in each of next 4 sts, inc in next st, [sc in each of next 8 sts, inc in next st] 5 times, sc in each of next 4 sts. (60 sc)

Rounds 10-20: *(11 rounds)* Sc in each st around. (60 sc)

Round 21: Sc in each of next 4 sts, dec, [sc in each of next 8 sts, dec] 5 times, sc in next 4 sts. (54 sc)

Start stuffing, adding more as you go.

Round 22: [Sc in each of next 7 sts, dec] 6 times. (48 sc)

Round 23: Sc in each of next 3 sts, dec, [sc in each of next 6 sts, dec] 5 times, sc in next 3 sts. (42 sc)

Round 24: [Sc in each of next 5 sts, dec] 6 times. (36 sc)

Round 25: [Sc in next st, dec] 12 times. (24 sc)

Fasten off, leaving a 20" (50 cm) long tail. (photos 11 & 12)

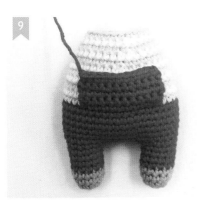

Front

Side

HAIR

Round 1: Using Color A, make an oval foundation chain of 6 stitches; starting in 2nd ch from hook, [sc in each of next 4 sts, inc in next st] 2 times. (12 sc)

Round 2: Inc in next st, sc in each of next 3 sts, inc in each of next 3 sts, sc in each of next 3 sts, inc in each of next 2 sts. (18 sc)

Round 3: Sc in next st, inc in next st, sc in each of next 3 sts, [sc in next st, inc in next st] 3 times, sc in each of next 3 sts, [sc in next st, inc in next st] 2 times. (24 sc)

Round 4: Sc in next st, inc in next st, sc in each of next 4 sts, [sc in next st, inc in next st, sc in next st] 3 times, sc in each of next 3 sts, [sc in next st, inc in next st, sc in next st] 2 times. (30 sc)

Round 5: Sc in each of next 3 sts, inc in next st, sc in each of next 3 sts, [sc in each of next 3 sts, inc in next st] 3 times, sc in each of next 3 sts, [sc in each of next 3 sts, inc in next st] 2 times. (36 sc)

Round 6: [Sc in each of next 5 sts, inc in next st] 6 times. (42 sc)

Round 7: Sc in each of next 3 sts, inc in next st, [sc in each of next 6 sts, inc in next st] 5 times, sc in each of next 3 sts. (48 sc)

Round 8: [Sc in each of next 7 sts, inc in next st] 6 times. (54 sc)

Round 9: Sc in each of next 4 sts, inc in next st, [sc in each of next 8 sts, inc in next st] 5 times, sc in each of next 4 sts. (60 sc)

Rounds 10-15: *(6 rounds)* Sc in each st around. (60 sc)

At the end of Round 15, fasten off.

Work continues in Rows

Row 16: Flatten the Hair piece *(with end-of-round joins at back)*; join Color A to 5th st from left (photo 13); ch 1, sc in same st as joining, sc in each of next 39 sts. (40 sc)

Rows 17-20: *(4 rows)* Ch 1, turn, sc in each st across.

At the end of Row 20, fasten off, leaving a 20" (50 cm) long tail. (photo 14)

SUSPENDER STRAP (Make 2)

Row 1: Using Color E, ch 29, sc in 5th ch from hook *(skipped ch-4 is buttonhole)* (photo 15), [sc in next ch] across. (25 sc) (photo 16)

Fasten off, leaving a 6" (15 cm) long tail.

HAT

Round 1: Using Color B, make a Magic Ring; 6 sc in ring. (6 sc)

Round 2: Inc in each st around. (12 sc)

Round 3: [Sc in next st, inc in next st] 6 times. (18 sc)

Round 4: Working in **back loops** only, sc in each st around. (18 sc)

Change to Color E.

Round 5: Sc in each st around. (18 sc)

Round 6: Working in front loops only, [sc in each of next 2 sts, inc in next st] 6 times. (24 sc)

Fasten off, leaving an 8" (20 cm) long tail. (photo 17)

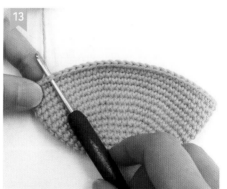

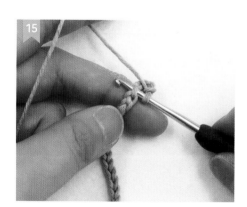
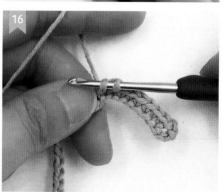

ASSEMBLY (use photos as guide)

Body: Using the long tail, sew the Head to Body, making sure the Face is the flat side of the head.

Arms: Sew the Arms to either side of the Body, one round below the neckline.

Hair: Position the Hair on the Head with the front bangs 13 rounds above the neckline. Using the long tails, sew in place. Do not finish off, continue with Eyebrows.

Face:

- Using the Dark Brown thread, embroider the Eyes about 10 rounds up from neckline and with 10 stitches between them.

- Embroider the Mouth about 7 rounds up from neckline.

- After sewing the Hair, using the tail, embroider the Eyebrows about 2 rounds above each Eye.

- With MC, embroider the Nose between the 9th and 10th round from neckline, between the Eyes.

- Using the Pink thread, embroider Cheeks between 8th & 9th rounds from neckline, one stitch on the outside of each eye.

Accessories:

- Sew each Suspender Strap on either side at the back between rounds 15 & 16, with 10 stitches between them. Cross the straps at the back and bring to the front. On the front, sew the buttons to each corner on the Bib. Fasten the suspenders to the buttons.

- Using Dark Brown Yarn, stitch the Felt Pocket to the Bib.

- Sew the Hat to the top of the Head.

GIRL

LEGS

First Leg

Round 1: Using Color B, make a Magic Ring; 6 sc in ring. (6 sc)

Round 2: Inc in each st around. (12 sc)

Rounds 3-4: *(2 rounds)* Sc in each st around. (12 sc)
Change to Color D.

Round 5: Sc in each st around. (12 sc)
Change to Color MC.

Rounds 6-7: *(2 rounds)* Sc in each st around. (12 sc)
At the end of Round 7, fasten off.

Second Leg

Rounds 1-7: Repeat Rounds 1-7 of First Leg.
At the end of Round 7, continue with Body. (photo 1)
Change to Color D.

BODY

Round 8: *(Joining Legs)* Working on Second Leg, sc in each of next 11 sts *(1 st remains unworked)*, ch 6; working on First Leg, sc in 2nd st (photo 2), sc in each of next 11 sts; working in ch-6, sc in each of next 6 ch (photo 3); working on Second Leg, sc in next st. (30 sc)

Round 9: Sc in each of next 11 sts; working in front loops only of ch-6, sc in each of next 6 ch (photo 4); sc in each of next 19 sts. (36 sc) (photo 5)

Round 10: [Sc in each of next 5 sts, inc in next st] 6 times. (42 sc)

Rounds 11-13: *(3 Rounds)* Sc in each st around. (42 sc)
Change to Color B.

Round 14: Sc in each st around. (42 sc)

Round 15: Working in **back loops** only, sc in each st around. (42 sc)

For the following rounds, alternate Colors C & D every round.

Round 16: [Sc in each of next 19 sts, dec] 2 times. (40 sc)

Round 17: Sc in each st around. (40 sc)

Round 18: Sc in each of next 9 sts, dec, sc in each of next 18 sts, dec, sc in each of next 9 sts. (38 sc)

Round 19: [Sc in each of next 17 sts, dec] 2 times. (36 sc)
Start stuffing, adding more as you go.

Round 20: Sc in each of next 8 sts, dec, sc in each of next 16 sts, dec, sc in each of next 8 sts. (34 sc)

Round 21: [Sc in each of next 15 sts, dec] 2 times. (32 sc)

Round 22: Sc in each of next 7 sts, dec, sc in each of next 14 sts, dec, sc in each of next 7 sts. (30 sc)

Round 23: [Sc in each of next 13 sts, dec] 2 times. (28 sc)

Round 24: Sc in each of next 6 sts, dec, sc in each of next 12 sts, dec, sc in each of next 6 sts. (26 sc)

Round 25: [Sc in each of next 11 sts, dec] 2 times. (24 sc)
Continue stuffing. Fasten off. (photo 6)

SKIRT

Round 1: Holding Toy upside down, working in the front loops of Body Round 14, starting at the back, join Color B to any st. (photo 7) ch 1, sc in same st as joining, sc in each of next 41 sts. (42 sc) (photo 8)

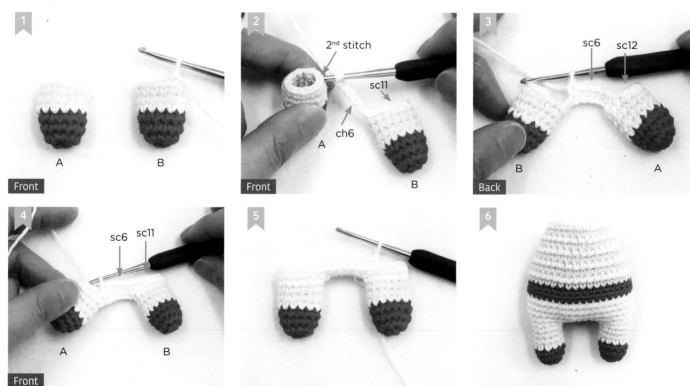

Round 2: [Sc in each of next 13 sts, inc in next st] 3 times. (45 sc)

Round 3: Sc in each of next 7 sts, inc in next st, [sc in each of next 14 sts, inc in next st] 2 times, sc in each of next 7 sts. (48 sc)

Round 4: [Sc in each of next 15 sts, inc in next st] 3 times. (51 sc)

Round 5: Sc in each of next 8 sts, inc in next st, [sc in each of next 16 sts, inc in next st] 2 times, sc in each of next 8 sts. (54 sc)

Fasten off and weave in all ends.

ARM (Make 2)

Round 1: Using MC, make a Magic Ring; 6 sc in ring. (6 sc)

Round 2: [Sc in next st, inc in next st] 3 times. (9 sc)

Rounds 3-4: *(2 rounds)* Sc in each st around. (9 sc)

For the following rounds, alternate Colors C & D every round.

Rounds 5-11: *(7 rounds)* Sc in each st around. (9 sc)

Stuff the Arm about ⅔ full.

Round 12: [Sc in next st, dec] 3 times. (6 sc)

Fasten off, leaving a 16" (40 cm) long tail. (photo 9)

HEAD

Round 1: Using MC, make an oval foundation chain of 6 stitches; starting in 2nd ch from hook, [sc in each of next 4 sts, inc in next st] 2 times. (12 sc)

Round 2: Inc in next st, sc in each of next 3 sts, inc in each of next 3 sts, sc in each of next 3 sts, inc in each of next 2 sts. (18 sc)

Round 3: Sc in next st, inc in next st, sc in each of next

3 sts, [sc in next st, inc in next st] 3 times, sc in each of next 3 sts, [sc in next st, inc in next st] 2 times. (24 sc)

Round 4: Sc in next st, inc in next st, sc in each of next 4 sts, [sc in next st, inc in next st, sc in next st] 3 times, sc in each of next 3 sts, [sc in next st, inc in next st, sc in next st] 2 times. (30 sc)

Round 5: Sc in each of next 3 sts, inc in next st, sc in each of next 3 sts, [sc in each of next 3 sts, inc in next st] 3 times, sc in each of next 3 sts, [sc in each of next 3 sts, inc in next st] 2 times. (36 sc)

Round 6: [Sc in each of next 5 sts, inc in next st] 6 times. (42 sc)

Round 7: Sc in each of next 3 sts, inc in next st, [sc in each of next 6 sts, inc in next st] 5 times, sc in each of next 3 sts. (48 sc)

Round 8: [Sc in each of next 7 sts, inc in next st] 6 times. (54 sc)

Round 9: Sc in each of next 4 sts, inc in next st, [sc in each of next 8 sts, inc in next st] 5 times, sc in each of next 4 sts. (60 sc)

Rounds 10-20: *(11 rounds)* Sc in each st around. (60 sc)

Round 21: Sc in each of next 4 sts, dec, [sc in each of next 8 sts, dec] 5 times, sc in next 4 sts. (54 sc)

Start stuffing, adding more as you go.

Round 22: [Sc in each of next 7 sts, dec] 6 times. (48 sc)

Round 23: Sc in each of next 3 sts, dec, [sc in each of next 6 sts, dec] 5 times, sc in next 3 sts. (42 sc)

Round 24: [Sc in each of next 5 sts, dec] 6 times. (36 sc)

Round 25: [Sc in next st, dec] 12 times. (24 sc)

Fasten off, leaving a 20" (50 cm) long tail. (photos 10 & 11)

Front

Side

HAIR

Round 1: Using Color A, make an oval foundation chain of 6 stitches; starting in 2nd ch from hook, [sc in each of next 4 sts, inc in next st] 2 times. (12 sc)

Round 2: Inc in next st, sc in each of next 3 sts, inc in each of next 3 sts, sc in each of next 3 sts, inc in each of next 2 sts. (18 sc)

Round 3: Sc in next st, inc in next st, sc in each of next 3 sts, [sc in next st, inc in next st] 3 times, sc in each of next 3 sts, [sc in next st, inc in next st] 2 times. (24 sc)

Round 4: Sc in next st, inc in next st, sc in each of next 4 sts, [sc in next st, inc in next st, sc in next st] 3 times, sc in each of next 3 sts, [sc in next st, inc in next st, sc in next st] 2 times. (30 sc)

Round 5: Sc in each of next 3 sts, inc in next st, sc in each of next 3 sts, [sc in each of next 3 sts, inc in next st] 3 times, sc in each of next 3 sts, [sc in each of next 3 sts, inc in next st] 2 times. (36 sc)

Round 6: [Sc in each of next 5 sts, inc in next st] 6 times. (42 sc)

Round 7: Sc in each of next 3 sts, inc in next st, [sc in each of next 6 sts, inc in next st] 5 times, sc in each of next 3 sts. (48 sc)

Round 8: [Sc in each of next 7 sts, inc in next st] 6 times. (54 sc)

Round 9: Sc in each of next 4 sts, inc in next st, [sc in each of next 8 sts, inc in next st] 5 times, sc in each of next 4 sts. (60 sc)

Rounds 10-15: *(6 rounds)* Sc in each st around. (60 sc)

Fasten off, leaving a 20" (50 cm) long tail.

SUSPENDER STRAP (Make 2)

Row 1: Using Color E, ch 31, sc in 5th ch from hook *(skipped ch-4 is buttonhole)*, [sc in next ch] across. (27 sc) (photo 12)

Fasten off, leaving a 6" (15 cm) long tail.

HAT

Round 1: Using Color B, make a Magic Ring; 6 sc in ring. (6 sc)

Round 2: Inc in each st around. (12 sc)

Round 3: [Sc in next st, inc in next st] 6 times. (18 sc)

Round 4: Working in **back loops** only, sc in each st around. (18 sc)

Change to Color E.

Round 5: Sc in each st around. (18 sc)

Round 6: Working in front loops only, [sc in each of next 2 sts, inc in next st] 6 times. (24 sc)

Fasten off, leaving an 8" (20 cm) long tail. (photo 13)

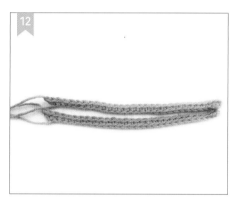

ASSEMBLY (use photos as guide)

Body: Using the long tail, sew the Head to Body, making sure the Face is the flat side of the head.

Arms: Sew the Arms to either side of the Body, one round below the neckline.

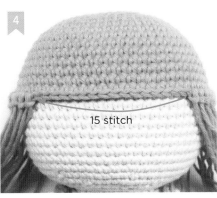

15 stitch

Hair Braids:

- Position the Hair on the Head, so that the front bangs are about 13 rounds above the neckline (photo 1), and sew in place.- Cut 30 strands of Color A into 8" (20cm) lengths.

- Attach 15 strands on each side of the Hair - with 15 stitches open across the front of the Hair. (photos 2-4)

- Braid the strands on each side, and using Color B, tie with a bow.

Face:

- Using the Dark Brown yarn, embroider the Eyes about 10 rounds up from neckline and with 10 stitches between them.

- Embroider the Eyebrows about 2 rounds above each Eye.

- With MC, embroider the Nose between the 9th and 10th round from neckline, between the Eyes.

- With Color B, embroider the Mouth about 7 rounds up from neckline.

- Using the Pink yarn, embroider Cheeks between 8th & 9th rounds from neckline, one stitch on the outside of each eye.

Accessories:

- Sew each Suspender Strap on either side at the back between Rounds 15 & 16, with 10 stitches between them. Cross the straps at the back and bring to the front. On the front, sew the buttons to Round 15 with 10 stitches between them. Fasten the suspenders to the buttons.

- Sew the Hat to the top of the Head.

DYLAN & DAOTA
the tall couple

DYLAN | Size (18½" / 47 cm)

YARN: HELLO Cotton Yarn

- Main color (MC) - Powder Peach (163)
- Color A - Cream (156)
- Color B - Sage (137)
- Color C - Mocha (125)
- Color D - Soft Gold (164)
- Color E - Dark Green (135)
- Color F - Brown (126)

HOOK: Size B-1 (2.25 mm) –
or size suitable for yarn used.

OTHER: Yarn Needle
Embroidery Needle
Toy Stuffing
Long Needle & Strong, Heavy-Duty Thread –
for Joints
8 mm Flat Dark Brown Button x 2 – for Eyes
13 mm Flat Wooden Button x 4 – for Joints
13 mm Flat Red Button x 2 – for Overalls
Water Soluble Marker
Grey Felt – for Pocket
Red Embroidery Thread

DAOTA | Size (18½" / 47 cm)

YARN: HELLO Cotton Yarn

- Main color (MC) - Powder Peach (163)
- Color A - Cream (156)
- Color G - Dark Salmon (112)
- Color H - Dark Beige (158)
- Color I - Chocolate Brown (168)
- Color J - Olive Green (172)
- Color K - Berry (108)

HOOK: Size B-1 (2.25 mm) – or size suitable for yarn used.
Size G-6 (4.00 mm) – for Girl's Hair

OTHER: Yarn Needle
Embroidery Needle
Toy Stuffing
Long Needle & Strong, Heavy-Duty Thread – for Joints
8 mm Flat Dark Brown Button x 2 – for Eyes
13 mm Flat Wooden Button x 4 – for Joints
10mm Flat Red Button x 2 – for Dress
10mm Flat Wooden Button x 1 – for closing Skirt
Floral Fabric – 22" (55 cm) wide by 6¼" (16 cm) long
Beige Felt – for Pocket
Sewing Needle and Thread

PATTERN NOTE

All pieces are made in joined rounds, unless otherwise specified.

SPECIAL STITCHES

Shell: Work 5 double crochet stitches in the same stitch or space specified.

Double Crochet Decrease (dc2tog): Yarn over hook, insert hook in next stitch and pull up a loop (3 loops on hook). Yarn over hook and draw through two loops on hook (2 loops remain on hook). Yarn over hook, insert hook in the following stitch and pull up a loop (4 loops on hook). Yarn over and draw through two loops on the hook (3 loops remain). Yarn over and draw through remaining 3 loops.

Back Post Single Crochet (BPsc): Insert the hook from back to front to back around the post of the specified stitch and pull up a loop *(2 loops on hook)*. Yarn over and draw through both loops on the hook.

Note: *A post stitch is worked under the top loops of a stitch, around the post (vertical part) of the stitch.*

BOY

HEAD

Round 1: Using MC, make a Magic Ring; 6 sc in ring. (6 sc)

Round 2: Inc in each st around. (12 sc)

Round 3: [Sc in next st, inc in next st] 6 times. (18 sc)

Round 4: Sc in next st, inc in next st, [sc in each of next 2 sts, inc in next st] 5 times, sc in next st. (24 sc)

Round 5: [Sc in each of next 3 sts, inc in next st] 6 times. (30 sc)

Round 6: Sc in each of next 2 sts, inc in next st, [sc in each of next 4 sts, inc in next st] 5 times, sc in each of next 2 sts. (36 sc)

Round 7: [Sc in each of next 5 sts, inc in next st] 6 times. (42 sc)

Round 8: Sc in each of next 3 sts, inc in next st, [sc in each of next 6 sts, inc in next st] 5 times, sc in each of next 3 sts. (48 sc)

Round 9: [Sc in each of next 7 sts, inc in next st] 6 times. (54 sc)

Round 10: Sc in each st around. (54 sc)

Round 11: Sc in each of next 4 sts, inc in next st, [sc in each of next 8 sts, inc in next st] 5 times, sc in each of next 4 sts. (60 sc)

Round 12: Sc in each st around. (60 sc)

Round 13: [Sc in each of next 9 sts, inc in next st] 6 times. (66 sc)

Rounds 14-22: *(9 rounds)* Sc in each st around. (66 sc)

Round 23: [Sc in each of next 9 sts, dec] 6 times. (60 sc)

Round 24: Sc in each st around. (60 sc)

Round 25: Sc in each of next 4 sts, dec, [sc in each of next 8 sts, dec] 5 times, sc in next 4 sts. (54 sc)

Round 26: Sc in each st around. (54 sc)

Round 27: [Sc in each of next 7 sts, dec] 6 times. (48 sc)

Round 28: Sc in each of next 3 sts, dec, [sc in each of next 6 sts, dec] 5 times, sc in each of next 3 sts. (42 sc)

Start stuffing, adding more as you go.

Round 29: [Sc in each of next 5 sts, dec] 6 times. (36 sc)

Round 30: Sc in each of next 2 sts, dec, [sc in each of next 4 sts, dec] 5 times, sc in each of next 2 sts. (30 sc)

Fasten off, leaving a 20" (50 cm) long tail. (photo 1)

BODY

Round 1: Using Color B, make a Magic Ring; 6 sc in ring. (6 sc)

Round 2: Inc in each st around. (12 sc)

Round 3: [Sc in next st, inc in next st] 6 times. (18 sc)

Round 4: Sc in next st, inc in next st, [sc in each of next 2 sts, inc in next st] 5 times, sc in next st. (24 sc)

Round 5: [Sc in each of next 3 sts, inc in next st] 6 times. (30 sc)

Round 6: Sc in each of next 2 sts, inc in next st, [sc in each of next 4 sts, inc in next st] 5 times, sc in each of next 2 sts. (36 sc)

Round 7: [Sc in each of next 5 sts, inc in next st] 6 times. (42 sc)

Round 8: Sc in each of next 3 sts, inc in next st, [sc in

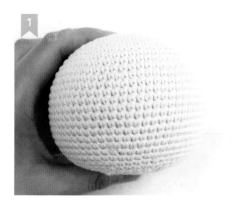

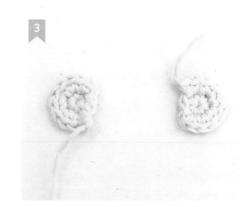

each of next 6 sts, inc in next st] 5 times, sc in each of next 3 sts. (48 sc)

Round 9: [Sc in each of next 7 sts, inc in next st] 6 times. (54 sc)

Round 10: Sc in each st around. (54 sc)

Round 11: Sc in each of next 4 sts, inc in next st, [sc in each of next 8 sts, inc in next st] 5 times, sc in each of next 4 sts. (60 sc)

Round 12: Sc in each st around. (60 sc)

Round 13: [Sc in each of next 9 sts, inc in next st] 6 times. (66 sc)

Rounds 14-17: (4 rounds) Sc in each st around. (66 sc)

For the following rounds, alternate Colors A, C & B every two rounds.

Round 18: Sc in each of next 10 sts, dec, [sc in each of next 20 sts, dec] 2 times, sc in next 10 sts. (63 sc)

Rounds 19-20: (2 rounds) Sc in each st around. (63 sc)

Round 21: [Sc in each of next 19 sts, dec] 3 times. (60 sc)

Rounds 22-23: (2 rounds) Sc in each st around. (60 sc)

Round 24: Sc in each of next 9 sts, dec, [sc in each of next 18 sts, dec] 2 times, sc in next 9 sts. (57 sc)

Rounds 25-26: (2 rounds) Sc in each st around. (57 sc)

Round 27: [Sc in each of next 17 sts, dec] 3 times. (54 sc)

Round 28: Sc in each st around. (54 sc)

Round 29: Sc in each of next 8 sts, dec, [sc in each of next 16 sts, dec] 2 times, sc in next 8 sts. (51 sc)

Round 30: Sc in each st around. (51 sc)

Round 31: [Sc in each of next 15 sts, dec] 3 times. (48 sc)

Round 32: Sc in each st around. (48 sc)

Round 33: Sc in each of next 7 sts, dec, [sc in each of next 14 sts, dec] 2 times, sc in next 7 sts. (45 sc)

Round 34: Sc in each st around. (45 sc)

Round 35: [Sc in each of next 13 sts, dec] 3 times. (42 sc)

Round 36: Sc in each st around. (42 sc)

Round 37: Sc in each of next 6 sts, dec, [sc in each of next 12 sts, dec] 2 times, sc in next 6 sts. (39 sc)

Round 38: Sc in each st around. (39 sc)

Round 39: [Sc in each of next 11 sts, dec] 3 times. (36 sc)

Round 40: Sc in each st around. (36 sc)

Round 41: Sc in each of next 5 sts, dec, [sc in each of next 10 sts, dec] 2 times, sc in next 5 sts. (33 sc)

Round 42: Sc in each st around. (33 sc)

Round 43: [Sc in each of next 9 sts, dec] 3 times. (30 sc)

Stuff the Body. Fasten off. (photo 2)

EAR (Make 2)

Round 1: Using MC, make a Magic Ring; 6 sc in ring. (6 sc)

Row 2: Inc in each of 5 sts. Leave remaining st unworked. (10 sc)

Fasten off, leaving an 8" (20 cm) long tail. (photo 3)

FINGERS (photo 4)

Index and Ring Finger (Make 4 – 2 for each hand)

Round 1: Using MC, make a Magic Ring; 5 sc in ring. (5 sc)

Rounds 2-6: (5 rounds) Sc in each st around. (5 sc)
At the end of Round 6, fasten off.

Middle Finger (Make 2 – 1 for each hand)

Round 1: Using MC, make a Magic Ring; 5 sc in ring. (5 sc)

Rounds 2-7: (6 rounds) Sc in each st around. (5 sc)
At the end of Round 7, fasten off.

Little Finger (Right Hand)

Round 1: Using MC, make a Magic Ring; 5 sc in ring. (5 sc)

Rounds 2-5: (4 rounds) Sc in each st around. (5 sc)
At the end of Round 5, fasten off.

Thumb (Left Hand)

Round 1: Using MC, make a Magic Ring; 6 sc in ring. (6 sc)

Rounds 2-4: (3 rounds) Sc in each st around. (6 sc)
At the end of Round 4, fasten off.

Little Finger (Left Hand)

Rounds 1-5: Repeat Rounds 1-5 of Little Finger (Right Hand). At the end of Round 5, continue with Left Hand & Arm.

Thumb (Right Hand)

Rounds 1-4: Repeat Rounds 1-4 of Thumb (Left Hand). At the end of Round 4, continue with Right Hand & Arm.

RIGHT HAND & ARM

Round 1: (Joining Fingers) Working on Thumb, sc in each of next 5 sts (1 st remains); working on Index Finger, sc in 2nd st, sc in each of next 2 sts (2 sts remain); working on Middle Finger, sc in 2nd st, sc in each of next 2 sts (2 sts remain); working on Ring Finger, sc in 2nd st, sc in each of next 2 sts (2 sts remain); working on Little Finger, sc in 2nd st, sc in each of next 4 sts; working on Ring Finger, sc in each of next 2 sts; working on Middle Finger, sc in each of next 2 sts; working on Index Finger, sc in each of next 2 sts; working on Thumb, sc in next st. (26 sc) (photos 4 & 5)

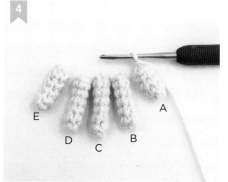

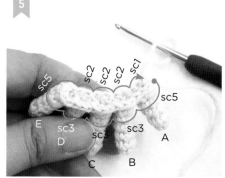

Round 2: Sc in each st around. (26 sc)

Round 3: [Sc in next each of next 3 sts, dec] 5 times, sc in next st. (21 sc)

Round 4: Sc in each st around. (21 sc)

Round 5: [Sc in next each of next 2 sts, dec] 5 times, sc in next st. (16 sc)

Round 6: Sc in each st around. (16 sc)

Stuff the Hand, adding more as you go.

Round 7: [Sc in next each of next 2 sts, dec] 4 times. (12 sc)

For the following rounds, alternate Colors B, C & A every two rounds.

Rounds 8-25: *(18 rounds)* Sc in each st around. (12 sc)

Stuff the lower Arm.

Round 26: [Dec] 6 times. (6 sc)

Round 27: Inc in each of next 6 sts. (12 sc)

Rounds 28-48: *(21 rounds)* Sc in each st around. (12 sc)

Stuff the upper Arm.

Round 49: [Dec] 6 times. (6 sc)

Close the last round with a needle. Secure and weave in the end.

LEFT HAND & ARM

Round 1: *(Joining Fingers)* Working on Little Finger, sc in each of next 4 sts *(1 st remains)*; working on Ring Finger, sc in 2nd st, sc in each of next 2 sts *(2 sts remain)*; working on Middle Finger, sc in 2nd st, sc in each of next 2 sts *(2 sts remain)*; working on Index Finger, sc in 2nd st, sc in each of next 2 sts *(2 sts remain)*; working on Thumb, sc in 2nd st, sc in each of next 5 sts; working on Index Finger, sc in each of next 2 sts; working on Middle Finger, sc in each of next 2 sts; working on Ring Finger, sc in each of next 2 sts; working on Little Finger, sc in next st. (26 sc) *(photos 6 & 7)*

Round 2: Sc in each st around. (26 sc)

Round 3: [Sc in next each of next 3 sts, dec] 5 times, sc in next st. (21 sc)

Round 4: Sc in each st around. (21 sc)

Round 5: [Sc in next each of next 2 sts, dec] 5 times, sc in next st. (16 sc)

Round 6: Sc in each st around. (16 sc)

Stuff the Hand, adding more as you go.

Round 7: [Sc in next each of next 2 sts, dec] 4 times. (12 sc)

For the following rounds, alternate Colors B, C & A every two rounds.

Rounds 8-25: *(18 rounds)* Sc in each st around. (12 sc)

Stuff the lower Arm.

Round 26: [Dec] 6 times. (6 sc)

Round 27: Inc in each of next 6 sts. (12 sc)

Rounds 28-48: *(21 rounds)* Sc in each st around. (12 sc)

Stuff the upper Arm.

Round 49: [Dec] 6 times. (6 sc)

Close the last round with a needle. Secure and weave in the end. *(photo 8)*

LEG (Make 2)

Round 1: Using Color A, make an oval foundation chain of 6 stitches; starting in 2nd ch from hook, [sc in each of next 4 sts, inc in next st] 2 times. (12 sc)

Round 2: Inc in next st, sc in each of next 3 sts, inc in each of next 3 sts, sc in each of next 3 sts, inc in each of next 2 sts. (18 sc)

Round 3: Sc in next st, inc in next st, sc in each of next 3 sts, [sc in next st, inc in next st] 3 times, sc in each of next 3 sts, [sc in next st, inc in next st] 2 times. (24 sc)

Round 4: [Sc in each of next 3 sts, inc in next st] 6 times. (30 sc)

Rounds 5-6: *(2 rounds)* Sc in each st around. (30 sc)

Round 7: Sc in each of next 8 sts, [dec] 6 times, sc in each of next 10 sts. (24 sc)

Round 8: Sc in each st around. (24 sc)

Start stuffing, adding more as you go.

Round 9: Sc in each of next 7 sts, [dec] 4 times, sc in each of next 9 sts. (20 sc)

Rounds 10-19: *(10 rounds)* Sc in each st around. (20 sc)

For the following 5 rounds, alternate Colors C & A every round.

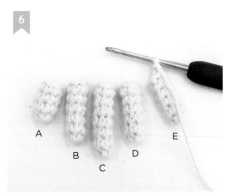

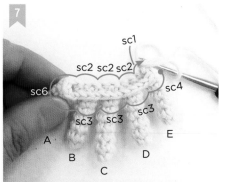

Rounds 20-24: *(5 rounds)* Sc in each st around. (20 sc)

Change to Color A.

Rounds 25-27: *(3 rounds)* Sc in each st around. (20 sc)

Change to MC.

Rounds 28-39: *(12 rounds)* Sc in each st around. (20 sc)

Round 40: [Sc in each of next 2 sts, dec] 5 times. (15 sc)

Stuff the lower Leg.

Round 41: [Sc in next st, dec] 5 times. (10 sc)

Round 42: [Sc in next st, inc in next st] 5 times. (15 sc)

Round 43: [Sc in each of next 2 sts, inc in next st] 5 times. (20 sc)

Start stuffing, adding more as you go.

Rounds 44-72: *(29 rounds)* Sc in each st around. (20 sc)

Round 73: [Sc in each of next 2 sts, dec] 5 times. (15 sc)

Stuff the upper Leg.

Round 74: [Sc in next st, dec] 5 times. (10 sc)

Close the last round with a needle. Secure and weave in the end. (photo 9)

SHOE (Make 2)

Round 1: Using Color C, make an oval foundation chain of 8 stitches; starting in 2nd ch from hook, [sc in each of next 6 sts, inc in next st] 2 times. (16 sc)

Round 2: Inc in next st, sc in each of next 5 sts, inc in each of next 3 sts, sc in each of next 5 sts, inc in each of next 2 sts. (22 sc)

Round 3: Sc in next st, inc in next st, sc in each of next

5 sts, [sc in next st, inc in next st] 3 times, sc in each of next 5 sts, [sc in next st, inc in next st] 2 times. (28 sc)

Round 4: [Sc in each of next 3 sts, inc in next st] 7 times. (35 sc)

Round 5: Sc in each of next 2 sts, inc in next st, [sc in each of next 4 sts, inc in next st] 6 times, sc in each of next 2 sts. (42 sc)

Round 6: BPsc in each st around. (42 sc)

Round 7: Sc in each st around. (42 sc)

Change to Color F

Round 8: Working in **back loops** only, Sc in each st around. (42 sc)

Round 9: Sc in each of next 9 sts, [dec] 3 times, [dc2tog] 4 times, [dec] 3 times, sc in each of next 13 sts. (32 sc)

Round 10: Sc in each of next 8 sts, dec, [dc2tog] 4 times, dec, sc in each of next 12 sts. (26 sc)

Round 11: Sc in each of next 22 sts, [dec] 2 times. (24 sc)

Rounds 12-14: *(3 rounds)* Sc in each st around. (24 sc)

Round 15: Sc in each st around, ch 5; join with sl st to first sc. (24 sc & ch-5)

Fasten off and weave in all ends. (photos 10 & 11)

OVERALLS

First Leg

Round 1: Using Color E, make a foundation chain of 33 stitches; join with sl st to first ch; ch 1, working in **back loops** only, sc in each ch around; join with sl st to first sc. (33 sc) (photos 12-14)

Round 2: Ch 1, sc in each st around; join with sl st to first sc. (33 sc)

Rounds 3-9: *(7 rounds)* Ch 3 *(counts as first dc, now and throughout)*, starting in 2nd st, dc in each of next 32 sts; join with sl st to first dc *(3rd ch of beginning ch-3)*. (33 dc)

Round 10: Ch 1, sc in each st around; join with sl st to first sc. (33 sc)

At the end of Round 10, fasten off.

Second Leg

Rounds 1-10: Repeat Rounds 1-10 of First Leg.

At the end of Round 10, continue with Shorts. (photo 15)

Shorts

Round 11: *(Joining Legs)* Ch 1, working on Second Leg, sc in each of next 30 sts *(3 sts remain unworked)*; working on First Leg, sc in 4th st, sc in each of next 32 sts; working on Second Leg, sc in each of next 3 sts; join with sl st to first sc. (66 sc) (photos 16-17)

Round 12: Ch 3, starting in 2nd st, dc in each of next 65 sts; join with sl st to first dc *(3rd ch of beginning ch-3)*. (66 dc)

Round 13: Ch 3, starting in 2nd st, dc in each of next 9 sts, dc2tog, [dc in each of next 20 sts, dc2tog] 2 times, dc in each of next 10 sts; join as before. (63 dc)

Round 14: Ch 3, starting in 2nd st, dc in each of next 18 sts, dc2tog, [dc in each of next 19 sts, dc2tog] 2 times; join as before. (60 dc)

Round 15: Ch 3, starting in 2nd st, dc in each of next 8 sts, dc2tog, [dc in each of next 18 sts, dc2tog] 2 times, dc in each of next 9 sts; join as before. (57 dc)

Round 16: Ch 3, starting in 2nd st, dc in each of next 16 sts, dc2tog, [dc in each of next 17 sts, dc2tog] 2 times; join as before. (54 dc)

Round 17: Ch 3, starting in 2nd st, dc in each of next 53 sts; join as before. (54 dc)

Round 18: Ch 3, starting in 2nd st, dc in each of next 7 sts, dc2tog, [dc in each of next 16 sts, dc2tog] 2 times, dc in each of next 8 sts; join as before. (51 dc)

Round 19: Ch 3, starting in 2nd st, dc in each of next 50 sts; join as before. (51 dc)

Round 20: Ch 3, starting in 2nd st, dc in each of next 14 sts, dc2tog, [dc in each of next 15 sts, dc2tog] 2 times; join as before. (48 dc)

Rounds 21-22: *(2 Rounds)* Ch 1, sc in each st around; join with sl st to first sc. (48 sc)

At the end of Round 22, fasten off and weave in ends. (photo 18)

Bib

With Shorts folded flat, working across the stitches on the front, join Color E in 6th st from edge. (photo 19)

Row 1: Ch 1, sc in each of next 14 sts. (14 sc) Leave remaining sts unworked.

Rows 2-9: *(8 Rows)* Ch 1, turn, sc in each st across. (14 sc)

At the end of Row 7, fasten off and weave in ends. (photo 20)

Overall Strap (Make 2)

Row 1: Using Color F, ch 35, sc in 6th ch from hook

6th stitch

(skipped ch-5 is buttonhole), [sc in next ch] across. (30 sc)

Fasten off, leaving a 6" (15 cm) long tail. (photo 21)

Finishing Overalls

- Using Red thread, sew the Felt Pocket to the Bib.

- Sew the Buttons to each corner of the Bib.

- Sew each Overall Strap on either side at the back with 12 stitches between them. Cross the straps at the back and bring to the front and fasten to the buttons. (photos 22 & 23)

ASSEMBLY (use photos as guide)

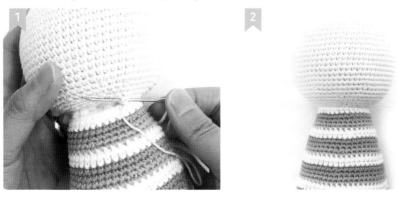

Body: Position the Head on the Body and using the long tails, sew together.

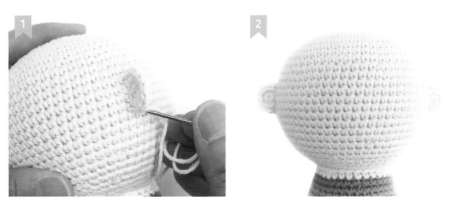

Ears: Position the Ears vertically on either side of the Head between Rounds 17-19, and sew in place.

117

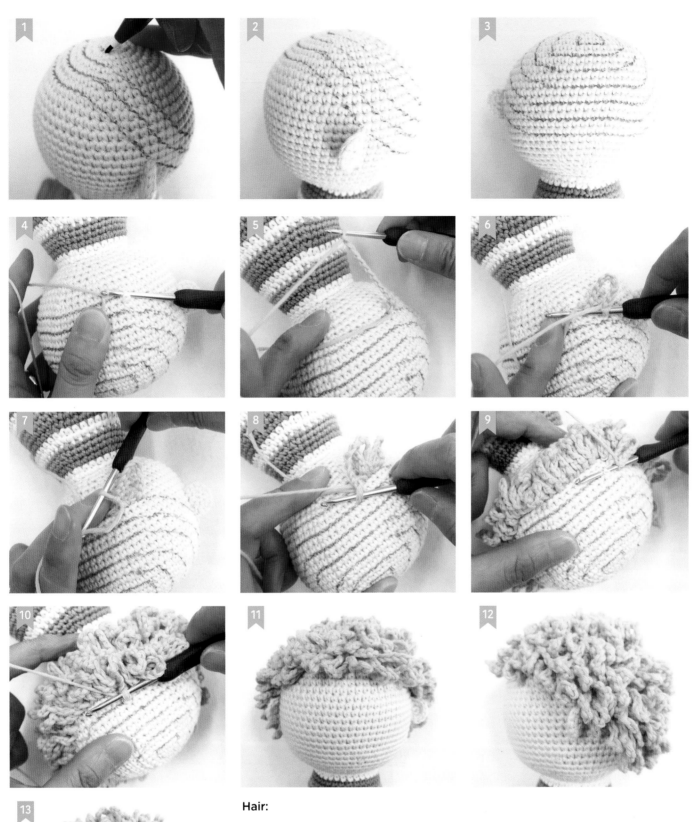

Hair:

- Using the water-soluble pen, mark the outline of the hair - between Rounds 9 & 10 at the front, and between Rounds 22 & 23 at the back.

- Draw more lines inside the outline at 2 round intervals. (photos 1-3)

- Starting on the outer line at the back, join Color D, ch 1, sc in same st as joining; ch 10, following the outlines and working in a spiral, [sc in next st, ch 10] around until all the outlines are completed. (photos 4-13)

Face:

- Sew the Eye Buttons on 14th round up from neckline, with 14 stitches between them.

- Using MC, embroider the Nose between the 13th & 14th round up from neckline.

- Using Color G (from Girl), embroider Cheeks between the 12th & 13th round up from neckline on the outside of each Eye.

- Using the Color C yarn, embroider the Eyebrows about 2-3 rounds above each Eye.

Arms: With Thumbs facing forward, place button-Arm-Body-Arm-button in order. Using a long needle, sew both Arms through the buttons onto the Body at the same time. The needle is inserted between Rounds 47 & 48 of the Arms, and between Rounds 41 & 42 on the Body. Sew 3-4 passes through all the pieces, making sure the Arms are properly secured.

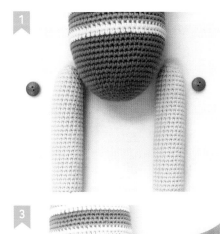

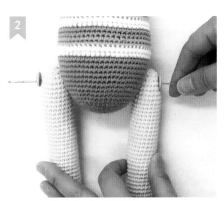

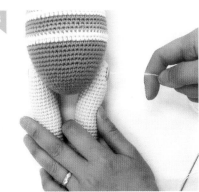

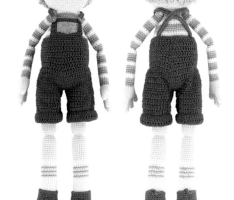

Accessories:

- Place Overalls on Doll and secure buttons.

- Place Shoes on feet.

Legs: With feet facing forward, place button-Leg-Body-Leg-button in order. Using a long needle, sew both Legs through the buttons onto the Body at the same time. The needle is inserted between Rounds 71 & 72 of the Legs, and between Rounds 9 & 10 on the Body. Sew 3-4 passes through all the pieces, making sure the Legs are properly secured.

HEAD

Round 1: Using MC, make a Magic Ring; 6 sc in ring. (6 sc)

Round 2: Inc in each st around. (12 sc)

Round 3: [Sc in next st, inc in next st] 6 times. (18 sc)

Round 4: Sc in next st, inc in next st, [sc in each of next 2 sts, inc in next st] 5 times, sc in next st. (24 sc)

Round 5: [Sc in each of next 3 sts, inc in next st] 6 times. (30 sc)

Round 6: Sc in each of next 2 sts, inc in next st, [sc in each of next 4 sts, inc in next st] 5 times, sc in each of next 2 sts. (36 sc)

Round 7: [Sc in each of next 5 sts, inc in next st] 6 times. (42 sc)

Round 8: Sc in each of next 3 sts, inc in next st, [sc in each of next 6 sts, inc in next st] 5 times, sc in each of next 3 sts. (48 sc)

Round 9: [Sc in each of next 7 sts, inc in next st] 6 times. (54 sc)

Round 10: Sc in each st around. (54 sc)

Round 11: Sc in each of next 4 sts, inc in next st, [sc in each of next 8 sts, inc in next st] 5 times, sc in each of next 4 sts. (60 sc)

Round 12: Sc in each st around. (60 sc)

Round 13: [Sc in each of next 9 sts, inc in next st] 6 times. (66 sc)

Rounds 14-22: *(9 rounds)* Sc in each st around. (66 sc)

Round 23: [Sc in each of next 9 sts, dec] 6 times. (60 sc)

Round 24: Sc in each st around. (60 sc)

Round 25: Sc in each of next 4 sts, dec, [sc in each of next 8 sts, dec] 5 times, sc in each of next 4 sts. (54 sc)

Round 26: Sc in each st around. (54 sc)

Round 27: [Sc in each of next 7 sts, dec] 6 times. (48 sc)

Round 28: Sc in each of next 3 sts, dec, [sc in each of next 6 sts, dec] 5 times, sc in each of next 3 sts. (42 sc)

Start stuffing, adding more as you go.

Round 29: [Sc in each of next 5 sts, dec] 6 times. (36 sc)

Round 30: Sc in each of next 2 sts, dec, [sc in each of next 4 sts, dec] 5 times, sc in next 2 sts. (30 sc)

Fasten off, leaving a 20" (50 cm) long tail. (photo 1)

BODY

Round 1: Using Color G, make a Magic Ring; 6 sc in ring. (6 sc)

Round 2: Inc in each st around. (12 sc)

Round 3: [Sc in next st, inc in next st] 6 times. (18 sc)

Round 4: Sc in next st, inc in next st, [sc in each of next 2 sts, inc in next st] 5 times, sc in next st. (24 sc)

Round 5: [Sc in each of next 3 sts, inc in next st] 6 times. (30 sc)

Round 6: Sc in each of next 2 sts, inc in next st, [sc in each of next 4 sts, inc in next st] 5 times, sc in each of next 2 sts. (36 sc)

Round 7: [Sc in each of next 5 sts, inc in next st] 6 times. (42 sc)

Round 8: Sc in each of next 3 sts, inc in next st, [sc in each of next 6 sts, inc in next st] 5 times, sc in each of next 3 sts. (48 sc)

Round 9: [Sc in each of next 7 sts, inc in next st] 6 times. (54 sc)

Round 10: Sc in each st around. (54 sc)

Round 11: Sc in each of next 4 sts, inc in next st, [sc in each of next 8 sts, inc in next st] 5 times, sc in each of next 4 sts. (60 sc)

Round 12: Sc in each st around. (60 sc)

Round 13: [Sc in each of next 9 sts, inc in next st] 6 times. (66 sc)

Rounds 14-17: *(4 rounds)* Sc in each st around. (66 sc)

For the following rounds, alternate Colors A, H & G every two rounds.

Round 18: Sc in each of next 10 sts, dec, [sc in each of next 20 sts, dec] 2 times, sc in next 10 sts. (63 sc)

Rounds 19-20: *(2 rounds)* Sc in each st around. (63 sc)

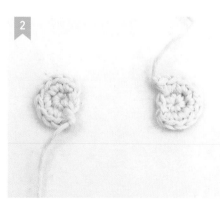

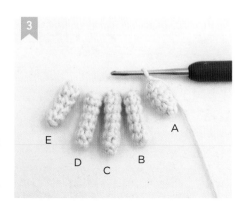

Round 21: [Sc in each of next 19 sts, dec] 3 times. (60 sc)

Rounds 22-23: *(2 rounds)* Sc in each st around. (60 sc)

Round 24: Sc in each of next 9 sts, dec, [sc in each of next 18 sts, dec] 2 times, sc in next 9 sts. (57 sc)

Rounds 25-26: *(2 rounds)* Sc in each st around. (57 sc)

Round 27: [Sc in each of next 17 sts, dec] 3 times. (54 sc)

Round 28: Sc in each st around. (54 sc)

Round 29: Sc in each of next 8 sts, dec, [sc in each of next 16 sts, dec] 2 times, sc in next 8 sts. (51 sc)

Round 30: Sc in each st around. (51 sc)

Round 31: [Sc in each of next 15 sts, dec] 3 times. (48 sc)

Round 32: Sc in each st around. (48 sc)

Round 33: Sc in each of next 7 sts, dec, [sc in each of next 14 sts, dec] 2 times, sc in next 7 sts. (45 sc)

Round 34: Sc in each st around. (45 sc)

Round 35: [Sc in each of next 13 sts, dec] 3 times. (42 sc)

Round 36: Sc in each st around. (42 sc)

Round 37: Sc in each of next 6 sts, dec, [sc in each of next 12 sts, dec] 2 times, sc in next 6 sts. (39 sc)

Round 38: Sc in each st around. (39 sc)

Round 39: [Sc in each of next 11 sts, dec] 3 times. (36 sc)

Round 40: Sc in each st around. (36 sc)

Round 41: Sc in each of next 5 sts, dec, [sc in each of next 10 sts, dec] 2 times, sc in next 5 sts. (33 sc)

Round 42: Sc in each st around. (33 sc)

Round 43: [Sc in each of next 9 sts, dec] 3 times. (30 sc)

Stuff the Body.

Fasten off.

EAR (Make 2)

Round 1: Using MC, make a Magic Ring; 6 sc in ring. (6 sc)

Row 2: Inc in each of 5 sts. Leave remaining st unworked. (10 sc)

Fasten off, leaving an 8" (20 cm) long tail. (photo 2)

FINGERS (photo 3)

Index and Ring Finger (Make 4 – 2 for each hand)

Round 1: Using MC, make a Magic Ring; 5 sc in ring. (5 sc)

Rounds 2-6: *(5 rounds)* Sc in each st around. (5 sc)

At the end of Round 6, fasten off.

Middle Finger (Make 2 – 1 for each hand)

Round 1: Using MC, make a Magic Ring; 5 sc in ring. (5 sc)

Rounds 2-7: *(6 rounds)* Sc in each st around. (5 sc)

At the end of Round 7, fasten off.

Little Finger (Right Hand)

Round 1: Using MC, make a Magic Ring; 5 sc in ring. (5 sc)

Rounds 2-5: *(4 rounds)* Sc in each st around. (5 sc)

At the end of Round 5, fasten off.

Thumb (Left Hand)

Round 1: Using MC, make a Magic Ring; 6 sc in ring. (6 sc)

Rounds 2-4: *(3 rounds)* Sc in each st around. (6 sc)

At the end of Round 4, fasten off.

Little Finger (Left Hand)

Rounds 1-5: Repeat Rounds 1-5 of Little Finger (Right Hand).

At the end of Round 5, continue with Left Hand & Arm.

Thumb (Right Hand)

Rounds 1-4: Repeat Rounds 1-4 of Thumb (Left Hand).

At the end of Round 4, continue with Right Hand & Arm.

RIGHT HAND & ARM

Round 1: *(Joining Fingers)* Working on Thumb, sc in each of next 5 sts *(1 st remains)*; working on Index Finger, sc in 2nd st, sc in each of next 2 sts *(2 sts remain)*; working on Middle Finger, sc in 2nd st, sc in each of next 2 sts *(2 sts remain)*; working on Ring Finger, sc in 2nd st, sc in each of next 2 sts *(2 sts remain)*; working on Little Finger, sc in 2nd st, sc in each of next 4 sts; working on Ring Finger, sc in each of next 2 sts; working on Middle Finger, sc in each of next 2 sts; working on Index Finger, sc in each of next 2 sts; working on Thumb, sc in next st. (26 sc) (photos 3 & 4)

Round 2: Sc in each st around. (26 sc)

Round 3: [Sc in next each of next 3 sts, dec] 5 times, sc in next st. (21 sc)

Round 4: Sc in each st around. (21 sc)

Round 5: [Sc in next each of next 2 sts, dec] 5 times, sc in next st. (16 sc)

Round 6: Sc in each st around. (16 sc)

Stuff the Hand, adding more as you go.

Round 7: [Sc in next each of next 2 sts, dec] 4 times. (12 sc)

For the following rounds, alternate Colors G, H & A every two rounds.

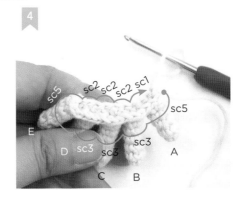

Rounds 8-25: *(18 rounds)* Sc in each st around. (12 sc)

Stuff the lower Arm.

Round 26: [Dec] 6 times. (6 sc)

Round 27: Inc in each of next 6 sts. (12 sc)

Rounds 28-48: *(21 rounds)* Sc in each st around. (12 sc)

Stuff the upper Arm.

Round 49: [Dec] 6 times. (6 sc)

Close the last round with a needle. Secure and weave in the end.

LEFT HAND & ARM

Round 1: *(Joining Fingers)* Working on Little Finger, sc in each of next 4 sts *(1 st remains)*; working on Ring Finger, sc in 2nd st, sc in each of next 2 sts *(2 sts remain)*; working on Middle Finger, sc in 2nd st, sc in each of next 2 sts *(2 sts remain)*; working on Index Finger, sc in 2nd st, sc in each of next 2 sts *(2 sts remain)*; working on Thumb, sc in 2nd st, sc in each of next 5 sts; working on Index Finger, sc in each of next 2 sts; working on Middle Finger, sc in each of next 2 sts; working on Ring Finger, sc in each of next 2 sts; working on Little Finger, sc in next st. (26 sc) (photos 5 & 6)

Round 2: Sc in each st around. (26 sc)

Round 3: [Sc in next each of next 3 sts, dec] 5 times, sc in next st. (21 sc)

Round 4: Sc in each st around. (21 sc)

Round 5: [Sc in next each of next 2 sts, dec] 5 times, sc in next st. (16 sc)

Round 6: Sc in each st around. (16 sc) (

Stuff the Hand, adding more as you go.

Round 7: [Sc in next each of next 2 sts, dec] 4 times. (12 sc) (photo 7)

For the following rounds, alternate Colors G, H & A every two rounds.

Rounds 8-25: *(18 rounds)* Sc in each st around. (12 sc)

Stuff the lower Arm.

Round 26: [Dec] 6 times. (6 sc)

Round 27: Inc in each of next 6 sts. (12 sc)

Rounds 28-48: *(21 rounds)* Sc in each st around. (12 sc)

Stuff the upper Arm.

Round 49: [Dec] 6 times. (6 sc)

Close the last round with a needle. Secure and weave in the end. (photo 8)

LEG (Make 2)

Round 1: Using Color A, make an oval foundation chain of 6 stitches; starting in 2nd ch from hook, [sc in each of next 4 sts, inc in next st] 2 times. (12 sc)

Round 2: Inc in next st, sc in each of next 3 sts, inc in each of next 3 sts, sc in each of next 3 sts, inc in each of next 2 sts. (18 sc)

Round 3: Sc in next st, inc in next st, sc in each of next 3 sts, [sc in next st, inc in next st] 3 times, sc in each of next 3 sts, [sc in next st, inc in next st] 2 times. (24 sc)

Round 4: [Sc in each of next 3 sts, inc in next st] 6 times. (30 sc)

Rounds 5-6: *(2 rounds)* Sc in each st around. (30 sc)

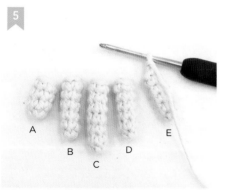

5

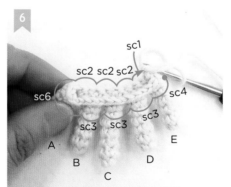

6

7

8

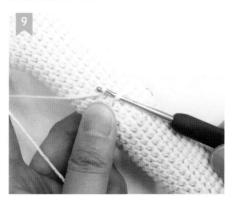

9

10

Round 7: Sc in each of next 8 sts, [dec] 6 times, sc in each of next 10 sts. (24 sc)

Round 8: Sc in each st around. (24 sc)

Start stuffing, adding more as you go.

Round 9: Sc in each of next 7 sts, [dec] 4 times, sc in each of next 9 sts. (20 sc)

Rounds 10-19: *(10 rounds)* Sc in each st around. (20 sc)

Round 20: Working in **back loops** only, sc in each st around. (20 sc)

Rounds 21-22: *(2 rounds)* Sc in each st around. (20 sc)

Change to Color MC.

Rounds 23-39: *(17 rounds)* Sc in each st around. (20 sc)

Round 40: [Sc in each of next 2 sts, dec] 5 times. (15 sc)

Stuff the lower Leg.

Round 41: [Sc in next st, dec] 5 times. (10 sc)

Round 42: [Sc in next st, inc in next st] 5 times. (15 sc)

Round 43: [Sc in each of next 2 sts, inc in next st] 5 times. (20 sc)

Start stuffing, adding more as you go.

Rounds 44-72: *(29 rounds)* Sc in each st around. (20 sc)

Round 73: [Sc in each of next 2 sts, dec] 5 times. (15 sc)

Stuff the upper Leg.

Round 74: [Sc in next st, dec] 5 times. (10 sc)

Close the last round with a needle. Secure and weave in the end.

Sock Detail (on each Leg)

Round 1: Holding Leg upside-down, working in front loops of Leg Round 19, join Color A to 12th st, ch 1, sc in each st around. (20 sc)

Round 2: Ch 1, sc in first st, ch 3, [sc in next st, ch 3] 19 times; join with sl st to first sc. (20 sc & 20 ch-3)

Fasten off and weave in all ends. (photos 9-12)

SHOE (Make 2)

Round 1: Using Color H, make an oval foundation chain of 8 stitches; starting in 2nd ch from hook, [sc in each of next 6 sts, inc in next st] 2 times. (16 sc)

Round 2: Inc in next st, sc in each of next 5 sts, inc in each of next 3 sts, sc in each of next 5 sts, inc in each of next 2 sts. (22 sc)

Round 3: Sc in next st, inc in next st, sc in each of next 5 sts, [sc in next st, inc in next st] 3 times, sc in each of next 5 sts, [sc in next st, inc in next st] 2 times. (28 sc)

Round 4: [Sc in each of next 3 sts, inc in next st] 7 times. (35 sc)

Round 5: Sc in each of next 2 sts, inc in next st, [sc in each of next 4 sts, inc in next st] 6 times, sc in each of next 2 sts. (42 sc)

Round 6: BPsc in each st around. (42 sc)

Change to Color K

Rounds 7-8: *(2 rounds)* Sc in each st around. (42 sc)

Round 9: Sc in each of next 9 sts, [dec] 3 times, [dc2tog] 4 times, [dec] 3 times, sc in each of next 13 sts. (32 sc)

Round 10: Sc in each of next 28 sts, [dec] 2 times. (30 sc)

Fasten off and weave in all ends.

Shoe Strap (Make 2)

Row 1: Using Color K, ch 14, sc in 5th ch from hook *(skipped ch-4 is buttonhole)*, [sc in next ch] across. (10 sc)

Fasten off, leaving a 6" (15 cm) long tail.

Finishing Shoes

- Attach a strap to the inside of each Shoe. (photos 13-15)
- Sew a button to the outside of each Shoe. (photos 16 & 17)

DRESS

Bodice

Row 1: Using Color J, make a foundation chain of 54 stitches; starting in 6th ch from hook *(buttonhole)*, sc in each of next 49 ch. (49 sc & ch-5)

Row 2: Ch 1, turn sc in each st across. (49 sc)

Row 3: Ch 1, turn, sc in first st, [skip next 2 sts, shell in next st, skip next 2 sts, sc in next st] 8 times.

Fasten off, leaving a 20" (50 cm) long tail. (photo 18)

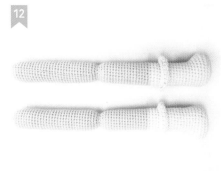

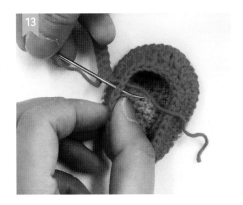

Bib

With right side facing, working on other side of foundation chain, join Color J to 19th st. (photo 19)

Row 1: Ch 1, sc in each of next 14 sts. (14 sc) (photo 20) Leave remaining sts unworked.

Rows 2-7: *(6 Rows)* Ch 1, turn, sc in each st across. (14 sc)

At the end of Row 7, fasten off and weave in ends.

Dress Strap (Make 2)

Row 1: Using Color J, ch 30, sc in 6th ch from hook *(skipped ch-5 is buttonhole)*, [sc in next ch] across. (25 sc)

Fasten off, leaving a 6" (15 cm) long tail.

Finishing Dress

- Prepare a piece of fabric - 22" (55 cm) wide by 6¼" (16 cm) long.

- Pleat or gather the fabric along the top width and sew to the Bodice. (photo 21)

- Fold the Bodice and fabric in half, and sew the edges together (center back seam), leaving an opening of about 2" (5 cm) at the top. (photo 22)

- Sew a ¼" (1 cm) hem around the bottom of the fabric. (photo 23)

- Using Color A, stich the Felt pocket to Bib. (photo 24)

- Sew a button to each corner of the Bib.

- Sew each Dress Strap about 6 stitches in from each end of the Bodice. Cross the straps at the back and bring to the front and fasten to the Bib buttons.

- Sew a button at the back to close the Bodice. (photo 25)

HAIR

Round 1: Holding 2 strands of Color I together, and using larger hook, make a Magic Ring; 6 sc in ring. (6 sc)

Round 2: Inc in each st around. (12 sc)

Round 3: [Sc in next st, inc in next st] 6 times. (18 sc)

Round 4: Sc in next st, inc in next st, [sc in each of next 2 sts, inc in next st] 5 times, sc in next st. (24 sc)

Round 5: [Sc in each of next 3 sts, inc in next st] 6 times. (30 sc)

Round 6: Sc in each of next 2 sts, inc in next st, [sc in each of next 4 sts, inc in next st] 5 times, sc in each of next 2 sts. (36 sc)

Round 7: [Sc in each of next 5 sts, inc in next st] 6 times. (42 sc)

Rounds 8-13: *(6 rounds)* Sc in each st around. (42 sc)

Round 14: Sc in each of next 2 sts, hdc in each of next 3 sts, dc in each of next 11 sts, hdc in each of next 3 sts, sc in each of next 5 sts, hdc in each of next 15 sts, sc in each of next 3 sts. (42 sts)

Fasten off, leaving a 20" (50 cm) long tail. (photo 26)

HAT

Round 1: Using Color H, make a Magic Ring; 6 sc in ring. (6 sc)

Round 2: Inc in each st around. (12 sc)

Round 3: [Sc in next st, inc in next st] 6 times. (18 sc)

Round 4: Sc in next st, inc in next st, [sc in each of next 2 sts, inc in next st] 5 times, sc in next st. (24 sc)

Round 5: [Sc in each of next 3 sts, inc in next st] 6 times. (30 sc)

Round 6: Sc in each of next 2 sts, inc in next st, [sc in each of next 4 sts, inc in next st] 5 times, sc in each of next 2 sts. (36 sc)

Round 7: [Sc in each of next 5 sts, inc in next st] 6 times. (42 sc)

Round 8: Sc in each of next 3 sts, inc in next st, [sc in each of next 6 sts, inc in next st] 5 times, sc in each of next 3 sts. (48 sc)

Round 9: [Sc in each of next 7 sts, inc in next st] 6 times. (54 sc)

Round 10: Sc in each of next 4 sts, inc in next st, [sc in each of next 8 sts, inc in next st] 5 times, sc in each of next 4 sts. (60 sc)

Round 11: [Sc in each of next 9 sts, inc in next st] 6 times. (66 sc)

Rounds 12-17: *(6 rounds)* Sc in each st around. (66 sc)

Change to Color K.

Rounds 18-19: *(2 rounds)* Sc in each st around. (66 sc)

Change to Color H.

Round 20: Sc in each of next 5 sts, inc in next st, [sc in each of next 10 sts, inc in next st] 5 times, sc in each of next 5 sts. (72 sc)

Round 21: [Sc in each of next 11 sts, inc in next st] 6 times. (78 sc)

Round 22: Sc in each of next 6 sts, inc in next st, [sc in each of next 12 sts, inc in next st] 5 times, sc in each of next 6 sts. (84 sc)

Round 23: [Sc in each of next 13 sts, inc in next st] 6 times. (90 sc)

Round 24: Sc in each of next 7 sts, inc in next st, [sc in each of next 14 sts, inc in next st] 5 times, sc in each of next 7 sts. (96 sc)

Fasten off and weave in all ends. (photo 27)

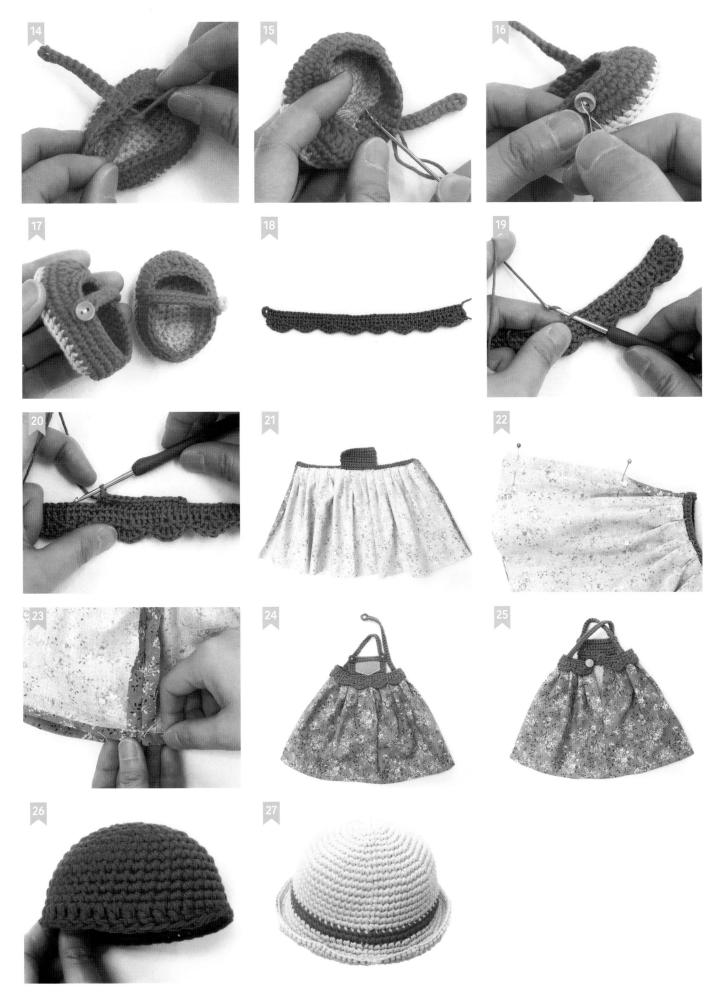

ASSEMBLY (use photos as guide)

Body: Position the Head on the Body and using the long tails, sew together.

Ears: Position the Ears vertically on either side of the Head between Rounds 17-19, and sew in place.

Hair Braids:

- Position the Hair on the back of the Head, so that the front bangs (dc-stitches) are about 19 rounds above the neckline (photo 1), and the back of the Hair (hdc-stitches) touches the neckline. Sew in place. (photo 2)

- Cut 48 strands of Color I into 16" (40cm) lengths.

- Holding 2 strands together, attach 12 pairs on each side - with 11 stitches open across the front of the Hair. (photos 3 & 4)

- Braid the strands on each side, and using Color K, tie with a bow. (photos 5 & 6)

Face:

- Sew the Eye Buttons on 14th round up from neckline, with 14 stitches between them.

- Using MC, embroider the Nose between the 13th & 14th round up from neckline.

- Using Color G, embroider Cheeks between the 12th & 13th round up from neckline on the outside of each Eye.

Arms: With Thumbs facing forward, place button-Arm-Body-Arm-button in order. Using a long needle, sew both Arms through the buttons onto the Body at the same time. The needle is inserted between Rounds 47 & 48 of the Arms, and between Rounds 41 & 42 on the Body. Sew 3-4 passes through all the pieces, making sure the Arms are properly secured.

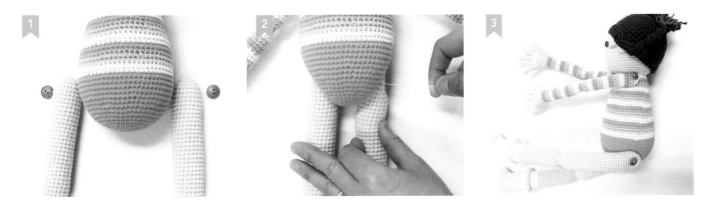

Legs: With feet facing forward, place button-Leg-Body-Leg-button in order. Using a long needle, sew both Legs through the buttons onto the Body at the same time. The needle is inserted between Rounds 71 & 72 of the Legs, and between Rounds 9 & 10 on the Body. Sew 3-4 passes through all the pieces, making sure the Legs are properly secured.

Accessories:

- Place Dress on Doll and fasten button at back.

- Place Shoes on feet.

- Place Hat on Head.